# Reroute the Preschool Juggernaut

*The Hoover Institution and Education Next Books gratefully acknowledge the following individuals and foundations for their support of this research on education policy and reform.*

LYNDE AND HARRY BRADLEY FOUNDATION

KORET FOUNDATION

EDMUND AND JEANNIK LITTLEFIELD FOUNDATION

BERNARD AND CATHERINE SCHWARTZ FOUNDATION

WILLIAM E. SIMON FOUNDATION

BOYD AND JILL SMITH

TAD AND DIANNE TAUBE FOUNDATION

JACK AND MARY WHEATLEY

# Reroute the
# Preschool Juggernaut

Chester E. Finn, Jr.

HOOVER INSTITUTION PRESS

STANFORD UNIVERSITY

STANFORD, CALIFORNIA

www.hoover.org

*An imprint of the Hoover Institution Press*
Hoover Institution Press Publication No. 572

First printing, 2009
16  15  14  13  12  11  10  09      9  8  7  6  5  4  3  2  1

Manufactured in the United States of America

The paper used in this publication meets the minimum requirements
of the American National Standard for Information Sciences—
Permanence of Paper for Printed Library Materials, ANSI Z39.48–1992. ∞

**Library of Congress Cataloging-in-Publication Data**

Finn, Chester E., Jr., 1944–
    Reroute the preschool juggernaut / by Chester E. Finn, Jr.
        p.  cm.
    Includes bibliographical references and index.
    ISBN-13: 978-0-8179-4991-4 (hardback : alk. paper)
    1. Education, Preschool—Government policy—United States. 2. Education, Preschool—United States—Public opinion. 3. Education, Preschool—Economic aspects—United States. 4. Public opinion—United States. 5. Education and state. I. Title.
LB1140.23.F56 2009
372.210973—dc22                                                      2009015883

For Alexandra and Emma, with love

# Contents

# Preface

Pre-kindergarten is one of the hottest topics in American education in 2009: Which children really need it? How many aren't getting it? Who should provide it—and at whose expense? What's the right balance between socialization and systematic instruction? Between education and child care? Where does Head Start fit in? What are reliable markers of quality in preschool programs? And much, much more.

Politics and adult interests loom large here, as always, but so does the country's earnest, overdue push to boost student learning, reduce vexing achievement gaps and strengthen our international competitiveness. Indeed, mounting attention to preschool seems, in hindsight, to be an inevitable corollary of standards-based reform of the primary-secondary grades.

If you find school reform a complicated challenge, however, wait until you wade into the turbid waters of preschool! And if you don't want to wade alone, by all means join me for a wetting in the pages that follow. We won't get much more than knee-deep—it's a fairly brief treatment of a large topic—but you may emerge with a basic understanding of the pre-K debate and the issues that drive and complicate it.

Although I've written what feels like a lot of books about education, this is my first sustained look at preschool. (As you will see, this domain is similar to K–12 in some ways but very different in others.) Fortunately, I've had plenty of assistance, beginning with my colleagues on the Task Force on K–12 Education at Stanford's Hoover Institution; they helped me get my mind around this subject and emboldened me to ask tough questions rather than succumb to the sentimental thinking that so often afflicts discussions of policy issues involving little kids.[1] As I proceeded, many others lent their hands, sending me studies, books, and articles, commenting on drafts, correcting my thinking (and sometimes my facts), and explaining mysteries. None, however, is responsible for whatever errors of fact or judgment may remain.

I owe particular thanks to Douglas Besharov, Bruce Fuller, Shan Goff, Marci Kanstoroom, Michael Petrilli, Robert C. Pianta, and Nina Rees, as well as Task Force members John Chubb, Eric Hanushek, Paul Hill, Caroline Hoxby, Tom Loveless, Terry Moe, Paul Peterson, Diane Ravitch, and Herbert Walberg.

The Hoover Institution generously provided all manner of support and encouragement, not least the publication of this monograph. I'm particularly grateful to director John Raisian and senior associate director Richard Sousa.

At my home base, the Thomas B. Fordham Institute, I benefited hugely from the patient precision of staff assistants Ali Clark and Mickey Muldoon, the cheerful willingness of my colleagues (especially Eric Osberg, Mike Petrilli and Terry Ryan) to pick up the slack while I labored on this project, and the continued forbearance of Fordham's board as I devote considerable chunks of time to such endeavors.

In the forbearance department, however, nobody surpasses my wife, Renu Virmani, recently joined in my affections (and her own) by two little pre-school granddaughters who don't yet have a lot of forbearance but who serve as a constant reminder of why this topic matters.

CHESTER E. FINN, JR.
*Washington, D.C.*
*March 2009*

# The Rolling Juggernaut

The campaign for universal preschool education in the United States has gained great momentum. Precisely as its strategists intend, many Americans are coming to believe that pre-kindergarten is a good and necessary thing for government to provide; indeed, that not providing it will cruelly deprive our youngest residents of their birthrights, blight their educational futures, and dim their life prospects.

The 2008 Democratic Party platform promised to "make quality, affordable early childhood care and education available to every American child from the day he or she is born," in effect offering a universal, entitlement-style program to the families of some twenty million youngsters under the age of five.

Twice during the presidential-campaign debates, Barack Obama termed early-childhood education one of his highest priorities, and even before serious planning got underway for an anti-recession "stimulus" package, he had pledged to this priority an additional $10 billion in annual federal funding. Sam Dillon of the *New York Times* termed Obama's offer "the largest new federal initiative for young children since Head Start began in 1965."[2] Obama's Education Secretary, Arne Duncan, is also a strong booster of pre-K education; as CEO of the Chicago schools, he set out to double the number of that city's preschool slots from 33,000 to 60,000 in response to "unmet demand."[3] (Duncan's—and Obama's—Chicago

1

contains about 40,000 four-year-olds.) During his confirmation hearing in January 2009, Duncan restated the key elements of the new administration's "Zero-to-Five" proposal, including "voluntary universal preschool quality enhancement"—whatever that may turn out to mean.

Congress is busy on this front, too. In June 2008, for example, just months after completing the belated Head Start reauthorization, the House education committee approved a new, $2.5 billion measure to assist states in elevating the quality of their preschool programs. The first few days of the 111th Congress brought a flurry of bills that ranged from child-care tax credits to state grants for additional pre-K programs, home visitation services, and more. The whopping economic-stimulus package enacted in February included $2.1 billion more for Head Start and $2 billion more for child care as well as additional funding for disabled pre-schoolers and some $54 billion in assistance to state and local education budgets.

In state capitals, meanwhile, many governors have embraced preschool in the early 21st Century with something like the fervor they brought to K–12 education reform during the late 20th Century. (Some say they've turned to the former because the latter has proved exasperating, expensive, and unproductive.[4]) Pre-K and kindergarten-expansion proposals topped their priorities in myriad "state of the state" messages in 2008. The previous year, thirty governors called for increased pre-K spending. The National Institute for Early Education Research (NIEER) hailed 2007 as a banner year, a time of "important milestones in expanding access" to state-funded preschool education, and declared that thirty-eight states now had such programs and that thirty of these had boosted their enrollments. "In Washington and statehouses across the country," wrote a *Wall Street Journal* reporter in August 2007, "preschool is moving to the head of the class." She termed the spread of free preschool education "one of the most significant expansions in public education in the 90 years since World War I, when kindergarten first became standard in American schools."

Preschool also looms large in the thinking of prominent education analysts and others who are alarmed by America's long-standing achievement gaps and doubtful that K–12 schooling alone can accomplish much gap-closing due to other powerful forces in the lives of children and families. In this view, school-centric initiatives such as the federal No Child Left Behind act (NCLB) are destined to fail because they don't start young enough and don't address those outside forces. Instead, they urge a "broader, bolder" approach that includes sharply increased investment in "developmentally appropriate and high-quality early childhood, preschool, and kindergarten education."[5] Arne Duncan was among many who put their names on a recent manifesto that argued this case.

This widening enthusiasm for universal or near-universal pre-K education is no accident. In the background, plenty of strings are being tugged and dollars spent. The *Journal* reporter quoted above ascribed much of the push to "a well-orchestrated campaign" that she traced to three individuals: "the research director of the Federal Reserve Bank of Minneapolis, a billionaire Oklahoma oil man and a foundation executive in Philadelphia."

The third person on that list is Susan Urahn of the $6-billion Pew Charitable Trusts, underwriter of much of the burgeoning advocacy work now underway in this field. Pew has made universal pre-kindergarten one of its top priorities, investing $50 million in this effort as of 2006. Plenty of other foundations and individual philanthropists are similarly engaged. As a result, a half-dozen energized, high-profile national groups now fill cyberspace, policymakers' inboxes, and committee witness lists. Many are Pew-aided, and many also have affiliates advocating away in sundry state capitals.

Prominent examples include the national group called Pre-K Now, with a fifteen-member staff headed by Libby Doggett, who previously worked for the National Head Start Association, and its clones in almost every state—organizations such as Preschool California, Voices for Ohio's Children, Winning Beginning NY, and Pennsylvania Partnerships for Children. Pushing hard on policy, research, and data is the Rutgers-based NIEER, which has two dozen staffers, a blue-ribbon advisory group, and generous funding from Pew and at least eight other private foundations as well as the U.S. Department of Education. Several influential business organizations, such as the National Association of Manufacturers and the Committee for Economic Development, have also climbed aboard the pre-K bandwagon, along with such other unexpected groups as the National Association of Counties and the National Governors Association.

Most have opted to pursue the "universal" model—prekindergarten for every four-year-old is their campaign slogan—rather than seeking more intensive intervention services targeted on a far smaller group of acutely disadvantaged children. Although the moral energy of the "universalists" derives from the claim that such a program will close educational gaps between America's haves and have-nots, their political strategy rests on the belief that enacting and funding any such program depends on mobilizing the self-interest of middle-class families who would welcome government-financed day care and an early educational advantage for their own kids. (The flaws in this approach reverberate through the following pages.)

Attention-getting books, most of them also underwritten by private foundations, have recently emerged on this topic, including Berkeley sociologist Bruce Fuller's perceptive and critical *Standardized Childhood*, partly financed by the Spencer and Packard foundations; Berkeley law professor David Kirp's (Pew-aided) *The Sandbox Investment*, which lucidly and passionately imparts the advocates' conventional wisdom; and (former *New York Times* education editor) Gene Maeroff's *Building Blocks* (subsidized by the Foundation for Child Development). Another formidable intellectual presence in this arena is James Heckman, a Nobel-Prize-winning economist at the University of Chicago.

One doesn't have to be a political savant to divine that this topic has traction with parents and voters as well as readers (and writers) of books and journals. Opinion polls typically find strong public support for state-provided child care and preschool—though such surveys rarely mention how it will be paid for. And when actual program proposals are put on the ballot—as in Florida's 2002 constitutional amendment mandating universal pre-K education—the electorate typically says aye. California's 2006 defeat of the "Rob Reiner initiative" was an important but rare exception. Despite heavy backing by public-sector unions and Hollywood celebrities, serious doubts eventually surfaced about the program's cost, its lack of targeting, the relatively few additional youngsters it would serve, and the threat it posed to extant independent providers of preschool and child care.

Such providers are among the many stakeholders with interests in these debates, interests that—to the exasperation of single-minded advocates—turn out to be less than perfectly aligned. Besides millions of small children and their parents, stakeholders include thousands of private for-profit and nonprofit operators of day care and preschool programs; any number of churches and their "ministries" and congregations; employers who provide or pay for child care (or are being pressed to do so); welfare and education reformers of every stripe; colleges of education; and an army of current child-care workers, many of them members of organizations such as the National Head Start Association, which claims to represent some 200,000 Head Start employees.

They comprise a diverse, volatile, opinionated, and self-interested tribe ranging from "that nice lady down the street" to huge commercial firms with franchises across the land to individual churches that make their Sunday-school classrooms available on weekdays for preschool. Moreover, what they deliver (and, for the most part, wish to continue delivering) is a blend of "day care," "preschool" and "pre-K" programs, some of it publicly financed and some private, some of it meager and some lavish, some of it cheap and some extremely pricey, as well as innumerable other arrangements for looking after and/or educating little kids—sometimes for an hour or two a day, sometimes from dawn to dusk and beyond.

The public schools and their teacher unions also have vital stakes in this field and its policy gyrations. The University of Maryland's Douglas Besharov and Douglas Call estimate that 90 percent of children supported by public pre-K funds in 2003-4 were enrolled in public-school-operated programs. (Pre-K Now says it's closer to 70 percent for state-funded pre-K.) Growing such programs would further expand school enrollments, system budgets, and union memberships.

Although it serves enormous numbers of small children, today's ragged armada of day care and preschool operators and programs, with their variegated eligibility requirements, uneven quality standards, and twisted funding streams, dismays advocates whose strategy hinges on propagating identical, universal programs designed to appeal to millions of parents and voters. That strategy relies on gaining the political boost that comes from offering John Q. and Sally Z. Public, both of them now working, the prospect that somebody else will pay for their child care, creating a new middle-class entitlement to government-financed services for their four- (and maybe three-) year-olds, wrapped in much hype about school readiness and social justice for the poor.

Because openly acknowledging this as their tactic would be embarrassing, pre-K advocates have devised the rhetorical device of asserting that universal programs will be *better* than programs confined to low-income families and disadvantaged kids. David Kirp summarizes—and endorses—this reasoning:

> Helping *all of us* and not just *them*—that division makes all the difference in the world. In theory, concentrating state pre-kindergartens entirely on poor children should help to close the education gap, and that would be a good thing. But a study carried out by two World Bank economists concluded that, when the voters effectively set tax levels, the poor are in fact *worse* off when a program is targeted, because the citizenry is willing to pony up much less money.[6]

As we shall see in the pages that follow, sophism is not too strong a term for such reasoning. Evidence from states with universal programs shows that they differ profoundly from the circa-1965, bells-and-whistles prototypes so often cited by today's advocates—precisely because that sort of boutique program is wholly unaffordable when large and broad based. We will indeed encounter problems with the big federal Head Start program, but those arise from its interest groups and ideology, not from its war-on-poverty-style income targeting. Kirp, Barnett, Doggett, and their philanthropic bank-rollers have got themselves into a misleading, even dishonest, place, using arguments about gap-closing to advocate universal programs that will not and cannot close gaps.

From the perspective of boosting educational achievement in general and the life prospects of needy youngsters in particular, there are better ways for America to proceed. These include highly targeted, heavily cognitive, intensive pre-K programs for the neediest children. Done right, focused on the right kids and melded with the right K–12 school reforms, pre-K education is a good thing. Universal pre-K programs of the sort pressed by most of today's advocates are not.

To track my journey, however, we must first address recent education changes that have brought unprecedented attention to the matter of school readiness; the hazy boundary between preschool and child care; and the extent to which American youngsters already have access to various forms of pre-K services.

Then we'll examine the shaky state of "standards" and "quality" in this field and the largely inconclusive nature of research and evidence as to "what works" for young children.

We next journey to Florida and Oklahoma for brief looks at two of America's most prominent examples of universal pre-K education, and we examine the iconic, four-decade-old, federal Head Start program. Thereafter, we probe the knotty (and in my view unresolved) matter of costs and benefits, and the fractious issue of alternative delivery systems. Which brings us, finally, to some conclusions and ideas for the path ahead.

# The School-Readiness Challenge

Confusion between pre-K or preschool education on the one hand, and "child care" or "day care" on the other, is real—and much exploited by advocates of universal programs. Nonetheless, I primarily focus in these pages on pre-kindergarten education itself, i.e., institutional arrangements for pre-K-age children that are specifically intended to prepare them to succeed in their subsequent schooling.

In today's world, that schooling is typically standards driven, frequently assessed, results based, and accountable. Some deplore such a mechanistic approach to teaching and learning, but it's here to stay—and has already yielded much alarming information about the weak performance of our children and schools. Most Americans now accept the *Nation at Risk* conclusions and NCLB premises that our K–12 achievement is inadequate, our school-performance gaps are too wide, our graduation rates are scandalously low, and too few kids emerge from our high schools truly proficient in essential skills and subjects.

Most observers also recognize that, while terrific schools do remarkable work with the pupils they have, many youngsters arrive in kindergarten with pre-existing learning deficits. For some of those children, the deficits are mild and can be dealt with by competent early-grade teachers. For others, the shortfalls are already so severe that they leave these hapless tykes gravely unprepared to flourish in today's more "academic" kindergartens; this means that—barring some change or miracle—those children won't likely be ready to prosper in first or second grade and beyond. They typically bring their learning deficits from disorganized homes in troubled neighborhoods, places where ill-prepared and overstretched adults, very often young single moms without much education of their own, offer babies and toddlers too little true conversation, intellectual stimulation, and cognitive growth.

Large bodies of research make clear that whether children successfully acquire literacy skills in the early grades of school correlates strongly with a half dozen "precursor" skills that are normally picked up between birth and age five. These include knowing the letters of the alphabet and their sounds; being able to write those letters—and one's own name; having what a panel on early literacy called "the ability to rapidly name a sequence of repeating random sets of pictures of objects (e.g., car, tree, house, man) or colors"; and possessing both phonological awareness and phonological memory, that is, detecting the elements of spoken language (e.g., syllables, words) and remembering spoken information.[7]

Middle-class kids with attentive, educated parents, grandparents, and other adults in their lives tend to acquire these (and many other) skills through the course of conventional child-rearing. But what about children whose lives lack a sufficient number of such adults?

Although school readiness is gauged primarily in cognitive and academic terms—and forms the principal focus of this discussion—it's not the whole story. Behavior and social development matter, too. Looking across a host of studies, economist David Figlio reports "consistent evidence that relatively disadvantaged low-income children misbehave at a greater rate than do relatively advantaged low-income children, and that this absolute gap increases over time."[8] It's well known that continual misbehavior, fighting, and "acting out" in school are accompanied by reduced learning, worse grades, less likelihood of being promoted, weak attendance, greater probability of getting sent to "special ed," and sundry other obstacles to educational success. If young children don't learn to behave before they reach kindergarten, that shortcoming could prove as detrimental to their schooling as not learning vocabulary, the alphabet, and the difference between squares and circles or big and little. Indeed, it could well prove *more* harmful, since teachers in the early grades may have greater success filling knowledge gaps than altering ingrained behavior patterns.

Whether cognitive or behavioral or both, "compensatory" education in the school itself is a costly, patchy enterprise, and while super-star teachers and ultra-high-performance schools exist, they are few and far between. The farther along a youngster is in school (and age), the greater the remedial challenge. Hence everybody will benefit if more can be done on the early-intervention front for the kids that need it most—provided, of course, that what's done is effective and that the effects last.

✦ ✦ ✦

Kindergarten success is itself a recent and still-disputed notion in American education. The (German) word means "children's garden," which is more suggestive of pleasurable play and natural development than of structured, rigorous, cognitive learning—and which accords with the strong view of many early-childhood educators that young kids should unfold like wild flowers rather than be cultivated like crops. This view has its origins in Piaget, in Rousseau, in the belief that small children should be sheltered from the stresses of adult society, and in the progressive-educator doctrine that learning is a natural act rather than the outcome of purpose-fully teaching a set curriculum. A modern exemplar of this view is Tufts University's David Elkind, whose warnings against "hur-rying" children begin with the belief that what is "developmentally appropriate" for girls and boys of pre-kindergarten age bears greater resemblance to play than to academics.[9]

Yet for better or worse, as part of our quarter-century-long quest to boost the performance of American K–12 education, kindergar-ten in state after state now has a bona fide curriculum and academic standards with a substantial cognitive emphasis, standards that (in a well-functioning system) harmonize with what follows in the primary grades.[10] So the question legitimately arises: what do youngsters need to know and be able to do upon *entering* kindergarten to maximize their chances of succeeding there and beyond? Where, if not at home, do they acquire those skills as well as the accompanying knowledge, habits, and capabilities? For children who aren't getting enough of those today, does the state have a responsibility to provide all it can? Although pre-K education (indeed, kindergarten itself in most juris-dictions) is not covered by compulsory attendance laws, does society nonetheless have an obligation to make it available to those who "need" it? If not, the chances may increase that, when some youngsters fall under NCLB testing requirements beginning in third grade, they will be deemed less than "proficient" in reading and math, not to mention the many other subjects and skills we expect schools to teach. This concern—plus the desire to start early to reduce achievement gaps among rich and poor, white and black and brown—underlies today's push for expanded pre-K education.

Understand, though, that institutionalized pre-K education is not the only conceivable way a concerned and compassionate soci-ety *could* tackle the problem of school readiness. Steps might be taken to boost the competence of parents and families within the home. Existing programs such as Head Start could be reconfigured into bona fide kindergarten-readiness programs. Or kindergarten itself might be reinvented, perhaps with an extended day, a longer year, and supercharged literacy teachers.

Kindergarten could last more than one year—for everyone or just for kids who need it. (The private school my kids attended inserted a "transition" year between kindergarten and first grade.) One might even picture a makeover of the full K-3 sequence, particularly to emphasize the essentials of early literacy and vocabulary, and to increase dramatically the amount of instruction in these areas for disadvantaged youngsters in the early grades. But such options entail changing the public-school system itself, so daunting a prospect that many people concerned with school readiness and early success prefer to conjure alternative institutional arrangements prior to entry into a stubbornly unyielding system.

This is a pity, because revamping the (universal and compulsory) primary grades might do more to meet the educational needs of disadvantaged children than adding voluntary programs in advance of schooling; and because (as we shall see below) today's schools often end up dissipating most of whatever gains are made in preschool.

In any case, K–12 schooling isn't where today's main early-education debate is taking place. That debate focuses on what should be done *prior* to kindergarten—and not on what could be done by reformulating current programs so much as creating new ones—for all kids, needy or comfortable, rather than just for youngsters who may need pre-K education.

+  +  +

My own views on early-childhood education have evolved, starting a decade ago, when Bill Bennett, John Cribb, and I wrote *The Educated Child: A Parent's Guide From Preschool Through Eighth Grade.*[11] We were known as conservatives and had, over the years, voiced doubts about excessive state interference in the lives of young children and their families. Our fundamental view was that education prior to kindergarten is a core obligation of parents and whatever arrangements they may make on their own and that any big moves into this sphere by government might actually weaken families. As education secretary in the late 1980's, Bennett had famously remarked on "the fallacy of the fourteen-egg omelet." If a chef can't cook a palatable 12-egg omelet due to a lousy recipe and miserable kitchen technique, he asked, why should we expect a better result from adding two more eggs to the pan? His point, of course, was that if schools are doing a poor job of educating kids during twelve primary-secondary grades, why would anybody think they'll be more effective if entrusted with two additional years of young lives?

When writing our guide for parents, however, we set about, almost off-handedly at first, in our "Getting Ready for School" chapter to itemize the knowledge and skills that young children should ideally possess upon entry into kindergarten in order to maximize their prospects there. Soon this list filled four book pages. Some of it was as obvious as knowing one's own name, dressing oneself, playing with other kids, and walking in a straight line. But we also found ourselves edging into more formal cognitive territory when we listed such skills as "retells little stories," "understands basic size words (e.g., big, little, long, short)" and "counts aloud to 10."

Nothing we set down felt like a long stretch; we didn't say that every child needs all of these skills by age five or else his/her life prospects are doomed; and we took for granted that many kids learn such things at home. But it started me thinking: what about boys and girls who don't acquire nearly enough of them at home— mainly poor kids and those from dysfunctional families and/or with ill-educated parents? Where will *they* obtain a decent portion of such skills before reaching kindergarten? It's an important question under any circumstance, and standards-based reform and NCLB have highlighted it.

Note, however, that I focused then as now on the youngsters who enter kindergarten clearly unready. There's no simple way to gauge their number precisely. The evidence indicates that it's around 10 percent, maybe 15-20 percent, of all children. It's certainly not 80 or 90 percent.[12] A lot of kids do get most of what they need at home or from arrangements that their parents make for nursery school, preschool, child care, grandparent care, and so on. It's misleading, even deceitful, to picture all five-year-olds at the threshold of kindergarten as woefully lacking the intellectual foundation on which to build a decent primary-secondary education. That is why America's current debate about universal pre-K is so wacky, so out of tune with most kids' real needs and circumstances. It's the children with major deficits who should command our attention.

Over the past two decades, much research has documented important knowledge and skill gaps among children when they enter school—gaps that show up in test scores, the extent of youngsters' vocabulary, and much more.[13] Reid Lyon, for example, estimates that "the average middle-class child is exposed to approximately 500,000 words by kindergarten" while "an economically disadvantaged child is exposed at best to half as many."[14] Other credible estimates find far greater differences. Whatever the size of the gap, those on one side of it need something more, maybe quite a lot; those on the other side do not, or at least not much.

Bruce Fuller has flagged the logical contradiction in pressing for a uniform program for all children while asserting that its purpose is to narrow gaps *between* children. When gap-closing is really the goal, a so-called universal program is almost never the best way to get there. He recalls, for example, early research on the acclaimed *Sesame Street* television program showing that, yes, it did benefit poor kids—but middle-class kids watched more of it and benefited more!

Anyone who has noticed the extraordinary time and care that upper-middle-class parents devote to talking and reading to their babies and toddlers, asking questions and pointing things out, providing gobs of (mostly positive) feedback—and taking pains to ensure a stimulating and varied environment—will have some sense of the obstacles awaiting a large-scale "institutional" program that seeks to deliver similar opportunities to youngsters who lack them at home. Waiting until age four, then spreading the available resources across all kids, the needy and the well parented alike, is simply not a promising formula for gap-closing or catch-up. Indeed, some prominent analysts, such as Todd Risley and Betty Hart, suggest that the shortfalls in the home environments of some infants and toddlers are so severe that their neural development and cognitive capacity may be permanently impaired by their fourth birthdays.[15]

Also troubling is the fact that, just as standards-based reformers at the K–12 level are better at identifying bad schools than at transforming them, pre-K advocates are far more adept at gauging and lamenting young children's learning gaps than at filling them—and keeping them filled. If the gaps are caused primarily by incapacity or apathy at home, it's obviously challenging to alter those circumstances and far from clear that readily replicable institutional programs can adequately compensate, at least not on a large scale and in lasting ways. If bad schools or malign non-school influences mean that pre-K gains don't endure through the primary (and secondary) grades, then the preschool experience, valuable as it may be in its own right, does not truly boost children's long-term prospects. That kind of gap filling resembles filling a colander with milk.

Meanwhile, some American schools are moving on their own to incorporate younger kids into their programs. Part of this reflects self-interest on the part of schools whose pupil counts are otherwise level or declining. Although U.S. elementary-secondary enrollments will rise by about 9 percent between 2004 and 2016, the on-the-ground picture is enormously uneven. Ten states, mostly in the Northeast, will lose K–12 enrollment during this period, even as growth tops 15 percent in another dozen states, almost all of them in the South and West. Teacher unions and ed schools have parallel interests in sustaining, even pumping up, the demand for their services.

But demographics aren't the whole story. Schools that take academic success for poor kids seriously are also finding that it's prudent to start educating them younger. When the celebrated Knowledge Is Power Program (KIPP) opened its first elementary school in Houston in 2006—by fall 2009 the organization will have 16 such schools—it began with pre-K precisely because the KIPP-sters had figured out that this is where they need to start with the disadvantaged children whose lives they seek to transform. KIPP CEO Richard Barth explains it this way:

> While we have had great success working with students in 5th through 8th grade, we have also recognized that by starting with children who are already one or two grade levels behind (by the 5th grade) we are signing up for a herculean task. Four years ago, we opened our first KIPP elementary school in Houston, Texas. We wanted to see what was possible when you start with children in pre-kindergarten. The results from our first two years, years in which our students finished kindergarten performing at the 1st and 2nd grade levels, convinced us that we needed to make this central to our growth in cities across the country. It is essential because we have committed to our kids and families that we are preparing our students for success in college and life, and the evidence is overwhelming that this will help us do just that.[16]

When E.D. Hirsch's respected Core Knowledge Foundation began in 1997 to develop a preschool curriculum sequence, it was for much the same reason. Hirsch had examined the French preschool system (*ècoles maternelles*), with its explicit cognitive curriculum for three- and four-year-olds, and found that it had positive and lasting effects on educational equity.[17] He wanted needy American youngsters to enjoy similar benefits. As he testified to a Congressional committee considering the reauthorization of Head Start in 1998,

> Children gain enabling pre-literacy and pre-arithmetic and other foundational learnings by having their minds deliberately formed through directed experiences in the home or in a preschool setting....The equity effects of French preschool increase cumulatively over time. Disadvantaged French children who attend preschool early rather than late increasingly close the equity gap as they progress through school. The comparative gains for these children are greater in 5th grade than they were in 1st grade — exactly the opposite pattern from fade out. What's the difference? A big one is that French preschools are accountable for explicit cognitive goals, and are followed by grade schools which are similarly accountable.[18]

Institutional settings, to repeat, are not the only places where pre-K learning can and does occur. Whether they're enrolled in preschool, day-care, or nothing at all, young kids spend most of their time at home, and much of what they do or don't learn will happen there. Many programs—local, national, international—therefore seek to help parents do better at prepping their own children for school. Prosperous Montgomery County, Maryland, for example, besides providing low-income kids with a formal pre-K program, steers all of its parents to myriad materials, programs, and resources by which they can do a better job of readying their daughters and sons for kindergarten.

Families across the land that seek such help can find it from many sources, including the Parents as Teachers program and Home Instruction for Parents of Preschool Youngsters, which began in Israel and now has sites in 25 states. Parents can also turn to any number of commercial products, non-profit organizations, and government offerings such as Even Start.[19]

These aren't patronized by poor families alone. Indeed, one reason for today's vexing gaps is that poor families, especially those that are both poor and dysfunctional, are *less* apt (or able) to avail themselves of such options than are their middle-class counterparts, increasingly obsessed as they are with prepping *their* kids for success in school and life. As childhood and adolescence last longer, our society seems to grow more child centered—and more inclined to act upon that priority not only by giving kids unprecedented goodies, freedoms, and deference but also by enveloping them in a ever-larger assortment of programs and services, many designed to boost their educational and career prospects by getting them an earlier start on mental development and learning. Hence all the "Leap Frog" toys and "Baby Einstein" recordings—and the emphasis on picking just the right preschool and other early-education opportunities. As Joseph Epstein recently wrote in an insightful essay on the contemporary U.S. "kindergarchy,"

> The craze of [excessive child] attentiveness hits its most passionate note with schooling, and schooling starts now younger and younger. When Lyndon Johnson began...Head Start, which provided the children of the poor with preschooling, so that they would catch up with the children of the middle class...the middle class soon set in motion a Head Start program of its own,

sending its children to nursery and preschools as early as is physiologically possible. Where one's child goes to school, how well he does in school, which schools give him the best shot at even better schools later on—these are all matters of the most intense concern.[20]

As we proceed, please keep this in mind: gap-narrowing for the poor won't be easy if the un-poor are also scrambling to preserve and magnify their advantage.

# Preschool or Child Care?

Besides preschool and school readiness, much public enthusiasm is tied to child care that offers working parents safe, affordable, and nurturing places to leave their young progeny. If taxpayers will cover those costs, so much the better, at least in the eyes of the beneficiaries. Although welfare reformers care more about access to day care per se than do preschool advocates, the latter energetically exploit the public's presumptive appetite for it to advance their own cause.

This topic would be far tidier and more coherent if a bright line divided child care from preschool. But of course there is no such thing. Most preschool programs serve a day-care function, too, affording parents a place where their daughters and sons will be cared for, given snacks and games as well as a cognitive boost, while they themselves work (or do chores or sip tea.) Such programs also provide "socialization" for youngsters who might not otherwise have much interaction with kids and adults outside their homes.[21] And many a day-care program serves an educational function, too, as staffers talk and read to their young charges, play games with them, or habituate them to useful school-readiness routines like standing in a line, saying please, and putting books back on the shelf.

Commercial operators of programs for young children commonly blur the line, suggesting to parents that they offer both early

education *and* child care—with a curriculum and learning goals
as well as flexible hours, naps, meals, before- and after-school cov-
erage, and other conveniences for working moms and dads. And
no doubt they do some of both. The firm that describes itself as
"the largest provider of early education and care in the nation" even
manages that straddle in its corporate name: KinderCare. So do
many smaller operators. A quick Internet search brought up Prep &
Play Preschool and Daycare Center, St. John's Daycare & Preschool
Center, and—covering all bases—Immanuel Lutheran Playschool,
Preschool, Pre-Kindergarten & Daycare.

Amalgams like these make practical sense, not just for marketing purposes but also in terms of meeting kids' needs and satisfy-
ing parents' preferences. What father would want his child simply
"looked after" during working hours if the youngster could also be
learning? No decent mother yearns for her toddler to be "taught"
but not cared for. And parents who work eight or more hours a
day need their kids tended for a longer period than pure preschools
traditionally offer.[22]

Blurring this line, in other words, works for program operators
and parents even as it confounds the policy discussion and politics
involved. (It also sorely complicates the quest for clear data about
who is getting what sorts of services from what sorts of providers at
whose expense.) For this tangled set of services and arrangements
taps into two separate policy domains and two different concepts of
"society's obligation."

It's self-evident that millions of working families who now
pay for child care themselves would welcome its public financing,
and it's also clear that some disadvantaged children could benefit
from solid preschool education. Pre-K advocacy organizations have
determined that their cause benefits from muddying the distinction
between those two sets of services, but policy makers ought to make

the line as clear and bright as they can. The United States already has a host of programs that address each of these objectives, and sound policy would start by appraising what they accomplish and how they might be improved.

The state plainly has an interest in upgrading its human talent across the board, as well as in narrowing harmful and unjust learning gaps and ensuring that everybody has a fighting chance to develop their intellect and skills to the maximum. Yet it's not self-evident that society has a compelling interest in paying for pre-K education except insofar as it demonstrably and durably accomplishes one or more of those objectives.

Nor is it obvious that the state has a compelling interest in paying for day care for the children of working parents unless they would be unable to work *without* that subsidy and therefore have to turn to welfare, crime, or some other socially costlier alternative.

In any event, these are not the *same* state functions, nor do they necessarily involve the same youngsters, nor are they best carried out in the same way. Child care for working parents, for example, needs to start with toddlers, if not infants. Perhaps intensive educational intervention for severely disadvantaged children does, too. But what's provided to these different populations of youngsters does not need to, and probably ought not, be identical. Neither social mission is a clear summons to "universality," considering that most working parents make their own child care arrangements and that many five-year-olds—thanks again to parents and those arrangements—arrive in school ready to learn what kindergarten teachers want them to learn.

# A Crowded Landscape

The porous border between child care and preschool confounds all efforts to count noses and confidently assign their owners to discrete program categories. A few key facts are clear, however. By 2006, reports the National Center for Education Statistics, 69 percent of four-year-olds and 42 percent of three-year-olds participated in "center-based," "pre-primary" programs of one sort or another. An additional 16 percent of four-year-olds and 28 percent of three-year-olds were being looked after in part by people other than their parents. (See Figure 1.) That means fewer than one-fifth of four-year-olds and one-third of three-year-olds were cared for solely by their parents.[23]

Unfortunately, the national data tell us little about the kinds of services these "center-based" and other non-parent providers are actually delivering, much less how good a job they're doing.

Before focusing on that problem, however, ponder this fundamental reality: roughly three-quarters of American three- and four-year-olds are already in a preschool or cared for in part by someone other than a parent. This fact has innumerable implications for society, including the obvious need to acknowledge that parents are no longer the exclusive caregivers and early-life educators in many households. At least as important is to understand that a large majority of families have already made their way to existing providers of

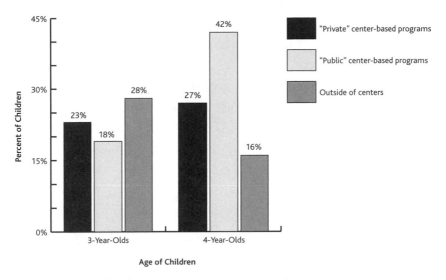

**FIGURE 1** Pre-kindergarten Participation, 2006

*Source*: Iruka and Carver, *2005 NHES Early Childhood Program Participation Survey*

such services at current public and private spending levels. Parents might welcome more program options and subsidies—but most do not absolutely need them.

Operators vary widely. The National Household Education Survey reports that, among three-to-five year olds who are cared for at least part-time by someone other than their parents, almost four-fifths take part in center-based arrangements. And we know that 28 percent of those arrangements are located in churches and synagogues, 23 percent in public school buildings (with 9 percent in private schools), and 31 percent in their own buildings, the last typically owned (or leased) by for-profit operators.[24]

It's impossible to know how many more parents might wish to arrange some sort of part- or full-time care for their young children. But keep in mind that a lot of parents stay home with them, at least part-time, because they want to. Among U.S. children under the age of six, only one-third of mothers work 35 or more hours weekly—and more than another third are not considered to be in the labor force. (Within the latter population, 68 percent have no "nonparental" care arrangement.)

Nobody can be sure how many of those moms are home because they believe it's best for their kids or how many might choose to work, or work more hours, outside the house if government would spring for their child care. Also unknown is how many might think differently if that care morphed into some sort of high-quality pre-K education. Surely some low-income families would make different arrangements if they had access to additional financial help. (The parents of 30 percent of four-year-olds in the lowest-income quintile report "no regular nonparental" care compared to 10 percent in the highest quintile.) Yet there's some evidence that demand may have leveled off well before the current economic downturn. Besharov and Call observe that:

> The influx of married women with children into the labor force largely came to a halt in the 1990s. About 30 percent of all mothers today still do not work outside the home. Include those who work only part time—most often less than 20 hours a week—and you will find that almost 50 percent of all mothers, and almost 60 percent of those with a child under three, are not in the full-time labor force.[25]

Note, too, that today's major push for universal pre-K is aimed at four- (and sometimes three-) year-olds, not at babies or toddlers. Also keep in mind that only 15 to 20 percent of those kids are *not* now participating in some sort of program or day care outside their homes.[26]

That's generally true of poor youngsters, too. Besharov estimates that 84 percent of *low-income* four-year-olds are already served by publicly financed preschool and/or day-care programs of some kind. Head Start is a key player here, enrolling about one-quarter of all black four-year-olds and a similar proportion of all low-income children. Also important to such families is the big federal child-care subsidy that was incorporated into the 1996 welfare reform act; that program—known as CCDF—now serves 1.75 million kids at a cost (exclusive of "economic stimulus" dollars) of almost $10 billion a year.[27]

Those large numbers don't satisfy the advocates, however. They fret that participation is still less than universal; that day care is not the same as preschool; that poor kids are more likely to be cared for by relatives (who may not themselves be well educated) than in centers; and that the center-based programs patronized by millions of families are of low quality.

They're at least partly right about quality, though they don't define it properly. (See discussion of the "quality conundrum" below.) Recognize, however, how much this public-policy slate has already been scribbled on. Scores of government programs, agencies, and missions intersect and overlap in the early-childhood domain. Some are licensing and regulatory offices tasked with ensuring that child care operators don't place their young charges in harm's way—and that they comply with states' often-exacting rules regarding class sizes, staff qualifications, fire escapes, wee toilets, and more. Other agencies are involved with family services, welfare and work programs for adults, the needs of disabled or severely "at-risk" children, and, of course, education itself. Florida's voluntary pre-K program is run by three separate state agencies and 31 county-level "early-learning coalitions," and delivered via 5,000-plus operators. (See discussion of Florida below.)

There's also a hodgepodge of federal, state, and local funding streams and regulations. Some programs are entirely taxpayer financed; others are wholly private; still others allow (or encourage)

| Federal Fiscal Year | Child Care and Development Fund | Temporary Assistance for Needy Families | Child/ Adult Care Food Program | Social Service Block Grants | Head Start | State-funded Pre-K |
|---|---|---|---|---|---|---|
| 1995 | $3,866 | $167 | $1,876 | $716 | $4,528 | - |
| 2000 | $8,191 | $2,478 | $1,910 | $187 | $5,972 | $1,964 * |
| 2005 | $9,380 | $2,309 | $2,111 | $241 | $6,842 | $2,837 |

FIGURE 2 Child Care and Early Childhood Education Spending (millions of 2005 dollars)

* Fiscal 1999 (2000 unavailable)

Source: Besharov, Higney, and Myers, *Child Care and Early Education Expenditures*

parents to "wrap" their own private-pay day care and "extended-day" arrangements around a publicly-funded core program.

Besharov and his colleagues found "as many as one hundred" separate federal and state programs paying for "some aspect of child care or early childhood education." The lion's share of such public support, however, flows through six programs, four of which focus principally on child care and two (Head Start and state-funded pre-K) on early education and school readiness. In 2005, Besharov estimates, spending across the six programs totaled $23.7 billion, of which nearly three-fifths was for child care and just 12 percent for the kind of state-funded education that is the pre-K advocates' top priority.[28] (See Figure 2.)

The advocates lament that so much of the money pays for child-care and hybrids rather than strictly for preschool. NIEER reports that total state funding of pre-kindergarten in 2006-7 came to $3.72 billion (almost a billion larger than Besharov's 2005 estimate) and that such programs served one million-plus youngsters or about 22 percent of four-year-olds and 3 percent of three-year-olds.[29] Even if accurate, however, those statistics mislead in their own way because far larger numbers of young children are served by—and much more money is spent on—care-oriented programs and Head Start. Except in advocates' eyes, there is nothing truly unique about state-funded pre-kindergarten. Let me say it again: more than two-thirds of four-year-olds and two-fifths of three-year-olds were in institutional pre-primary programs of some sort in 2006. Within those big totals, 27 percent of four-year-olds and 23 percent of three-year-olds took part in private programs,[30] while 42 percent and 19 percent, respectively, were in public ones (including Head Start). In other words, existing public programs of various kinds already serve almost twice as many four-year-olds and *six times* as many three-year-olds as NIEER finds in state funded pre-K programs.

Because so many families have already worked something out for their kids and so many levels of government are involved in so many ways, we don't have to choose between new programs and no program. America is plainly not starting from scratch. Yet that reality compounds the policy dilemmas: Should government henceforth leave families and private providers alone to function freely via markets with the help of existing programs and subsidies? Should it further subsidize purchasers, perhaps through vouchers or tax credits, so that more of them can exercise choices in the private market? Or should it displace or replace, or add to or make over, this intricate network of arrangements with a new or expanded set of publicly provided services for some or all children? And how much attention should it pay to program quality—provided, that is, that the laudable yet elusive concept of quality can be properly defined and appraised?

# The Quality Conundrum

What is "high-quality" preschool? Nobody wants little kids placed in shoddy programs. But a raging dispute surrounds the definition of quality in this field, and the dominant versions are ill suited to the modern kindergarten-readiness era. Those who would "leave no toddler behind" have enormous difficulty spelling out the preschool equivalent of what, in the K–12 sector, we typically term "proficiency." And they seem loath to devise and deploy suitable measures of progress toward that result.

Indeed, I sometimes feel as if pre-K advocates inhabit a different universe from the K–12 policy world where I mainly dwell. Two fixed stars are missing altogether: States have no constitutional duty to provide their citizens with preschool education (or didn't until advocates persuaded Georgia and Florida to amend their constitutions to create such an obligation.) And no state has made pre-K education compulsory for young children, as every state does for those of school age. Pre-K education thus remains for the most part optional from the standpoint of both providers and consumers—an incalculable difference from the primary-secondary arena.

Governance and regulation differ, too. While K–12 education now places heavy emphasis on state-prescribed academic standards, assessments, and outcomes (as well as continued—I would say excessive—regulation of inputs and delivery systems), pre-K education remains fixated on resources, services, licenses, and credentials.

Most early-education experts are similarly fixated. Indeed, the pre-K policy arena still functions for the most part in a pre-Coleman world of spending levels, staffing ratios, and college degrees rather than cognitive expectations, pupil assessments, and results-based accountability.[31] Nor are the data on outcomes much good. Even where states try to prescribe the desired results or regulate the curricular content of pre-K programs, except for Florida they end up with scant information on whether that content is being successfully imparted to small children, much less whether it's retained later. The situation is hard to rectify, too, because assessment in this domain is underdeveloped and heavily disputed, because many early-childhood educators care more about non-cognitive elements of child development and because (as in K–12 education) existing providers are loath to be judged by the results of their efforts.

In partial contrast with the K–12 world's familiar distinction between school inputs and student achievement, pre-K analysts tend to distinguish between two broad genres of quality criteria: "structural" quality, which deals primarily with such organizational characteristics of a program—I usually term them "inputs"—as child-staff ratios, class sizes, teacher credentials, and physical safety; and "process" quality, which focuses on interactions among children and staff, environment, and other kids.[32] There's a presumption (with good research validating it) that such "process" interactions, when skillfully and regularly deployed in classrooms, are associated with more cognitively developed and school-ready youngsters. As a recent report by The Albert Shanker Institute notes, "Of particular importance is the quality of instruction, which appears to have a vital, lasting effect on building children's cognitive and social skills through the elementary school years."[33]

In the present education-policy environment, with its heavy cognitive emphasis and school-readiness focus, it would be valuable to add a third metric for judging quality: pre-K programs' actual results gauged in terms of their "graduates'" readiness for academic success in kindergarten and beyond. Today, however, we're a long way from acceptance of that view across much of the early-childhood community. (Florida is again an exception—but many experts scorn the Sunshine State approach.) In fact, none of the three most widely used sets of "quality" criteria in this field pays much heed to learning outcomes; and by and large, they don't do very well by "process" measures, either. They mostly focus on "structural" (i.e., input) considerations.

For decades, most experts have relied heavily on a metric called the Early Childhood Environment Rating Scale (ECERS), developed by Thelma Harms and the University of North Carolina's Frank Porter Graham Child Development Institute. Its stated purpose is to "assess group programs for children of preschool through kindergarten," and the current version clumps 43 program characteristics into seven categories. A few elements deal with interactions between preschoolers and their teachers but none deals directly with outcomes or school readiness. Most focus on a center's resources, routines, staffing, and activities.

As Abt Associates' Jean Layzer and Barbara Goodson point out, the ECERS scale "was originally developed as a tool that centers could use for self-assessment to target areas for improvement…[and] reflects a generous expansive vision of what is necessary to create a comfortable and nurturing center environment for children." ECERS was not, however, designed with an education-outcomes orientation or kindergarten-readiness emphasis. Indeed, it was not created with any cognitive or curricular focus, and it neglects or undervalues elements of school readiness that matter in kindergarten. "For example," say Layzer and Goodson, "the four

ECERS items that measure the extent to which the environment meets adults' needs made the same contribution to the [center's] total score as the four items that assess the quality of children's language and reasoning experiences. As a result, it is possible [using ECERS] to give a highly favorable rating to programs that offer minimal support for language and literacy acquisition."[34]

Also quite influential in early-childhood program evaluations and quality judgments are the standards of the National Association for the Education of Young Children (NAEYC), a voluntary accrediting body that has given its stamp of approval to thousands of such centers. For many years, its standards were almost entirely structural. Today, they span ten areas from curriculum to management. Here's a sampler of what NAEYC looks for in programs seeking its approval:

> Curriculum: ...Children are provided opportunities to experience oral and written communication in a language their family uses or understands....Children have varied opportunities to develop vocabulary through conversations, experiences, field trips, and books....
>
> Teaching: Teaching staff create and maintain a setting in which children of differing abilities can progress, with guidance, toward increasing levels of autonomy, responsibility, and empathy....Teachers notice patterns in children's challenging behaviors to provide thoughtful, consistent, and individualized responses.
>
> Teachers: All teachers have a minimum of an associate's degree or equivalent. At least 75 percent of teachers have a minimum of a baccalaureate degree....All teaching staff have specialized college-level course work and/or professional development training that prepares them to work with children and families of diverse races, cultures, and languages.

Physical environment: There is a minimum of 35 square feet of usable space per child in each of the primary indoor activity areas....Toilets, drinking water, and hand-washing facilities are within 40 feet of the indoor areas that children use....

Leadership and management: The program administrator responds proactively to changing conditions to enhance program quality....The program administrator and other program leaders systematically support an organizational climate that fosters trust, collaboration, and inclusion.

Such criteria appear wholly worthy on their face, almost unimpeachable (once you get past a touch of political correctness). Who would want a three- or four-year-old child in any other sort of environment? No one credibly claims that environmental and structural considerations are wholly irrelevant, since no one thinks it's good for little kids to be in unsanitary, chilly, or hot places or in the hands of adults with bad habits or police records. It's worth noting, too, that the current NAEYC standards, adopted in 2006, are far more explicit than their predecessors regarding curriculum, assessment, and cognitive development.

Yet even after all the revising and updating, the standards are still chiefly concerned with resources, services, aspirations, and activities. They do not convey any explicit sense of what young children need to learn or how to determine whether they've learned it. Scant attention is paid to process considerations and less to cognitive outcomes. And some of the NAEYC standards' most-cited-and-deferred-to elements—such as pre-K teachers possessing bachelor's degrees—have at best a mixed and nebulous bearing on student learning.[35]

Learning, however, is not the overriding consideration. One pores in vain through NAEYC's standards in search of any clear statement that the mission of early education is to prepare children to thrive in kindergarten and beyond. Rather, the stated purpose is to ensure that accredited programs "advance children's growth," are "consistently nurturing and filled with learning opportunities," and so on.

While NAEYC and ECERS focus on individual programs and centers, Pew-supported NIEER concentrates on state policies. It evaluates them against ten "quality standards," eight of which pertain to resources and services: class-size limits and kid-to-teacher ratios, staff credentials, meals, referral services, and so forth. The two that deal with content and assessment are both sound as far as they go. One says that the "National Education Goals Panel content areas covered by state learning standards for preschool-age children must be comprehensive." The other says that "Site visits must be used to demonstrate ongoing adherence to state program standards."

But look again. The site-visit standard says nothing about what those "state program standards" should be and is mute about educational outcomes or how to gauge them. This is classic "compliance" language, not "results" language.

The content-areas standard—invoking the National Education Goals Panel specifications circa 1991—isn't bad. (Those content areas, by the way, are "children's physical well-being and motor development, social-emotional development, approaches toward learning, language development, and cognition and general knowledge.") Note, however, that the text says only that states should have "comprehensive" learning standards in those areas. It doesn't say what the standards should include or that the state must have a mechanism to determine whether its pre-K programs in fact meet them.

Ironically, the Goals Panel itself recommended almost two decades ago that states adopt comprehensive assessment systems to determine children's readiness for school.[36] But nothing like that has made it into the NIEER policy check-list for state pre-K programs.

Given such flabby criteria for quality, we shouldn't be surprised that relatively few studies of early childhood programs do a great job of appraising their educational efficacy. Many don't even try. In 2006, Martha Zaslow and colleagues examined 65 studies of child-care quality published over the previous quarter century. Barely half of them even focused on "language development" and/or "cognition and general knowledge," and among those that did, more than one-third had methodological shortcomings.[37]

In short: although it's been trying to make its way into the 21st Century, post-Coleman understanding that education quality is in the end not about what goes into a program or happens there but about the results that are achieved, the pre-K world has not yet reached this destination. It displays widening recognition that its programs and policies *ought* to have a standards-and-results orientation. At the same time, it harbors continuing arguments over what those standards ought to be, how to assess whether they're being met, and whether anyone is or should be held to account for producing success or failure.

Without widespread use of agreed-upon quality metrics that address program outcomes and school readiness, it's no surprise that available data about early-childhood offerings, operators, and participation rates are so murky with regard to "education" versus "child care" as well as program effectiveness and cost compared with benefit. Economists David Blau and Janet Currie, after reviewing much of the relevant literature, found that while "process quality is more closely related to child development than structural [i.e., input] quality…there are no nationally representative data available on process measures. Researchers must rely on structural measures under the assumption that the two types of quality are related. Complicating matters further is the failure of the U.S. child care data collection system to collect quality data on a regular basis."[38]

Other analysts voice similar doubts about the established quality criteria in this field. Robert C. Pianta, dean of the University of Virginia school of education and a developer of assessment methods that have yielded empirical data on thousands of pre-K classrooms, says that what actually makes a difference in pre-school learning is well established but that the usual criteria bear scant relationship to it. "The evidence," he says, "is quite clear that it is the teacher's *implementation* of a curriculum, through both social and instructional interactions with children, that produces effects on student learning." By that he means teachers who "strategically weave instruction into activities that give children choices to explore and play," including "explicit instruction in certain key skills; responsive feedback; and verbal engagement/stimulation."[39]

When Pianta applies that definition of quality to today's pre-K programs, he doesn't find much of it. His research team determined that "only about 25 percent of classrooms serving 4-year-olds provided students with the high levels of emotional and instructional support that are needed....Unfortunately, exposure to gap-closing classroom quality, although highly desirable from nearly every perspective imaginable, is not a regular feature of early schooling and even less likely for children in poverty."[40]

This is not good news for advocates of universal preschooling. What Pianta is saying is that when educationally relevant "process" criteria are systematically deployed in reviewing existing programs, high-quality pre-kindergarten turns out to be a rarity. Worse, the criteria that are more commonly used—the "structural" kind, with their emphasis on inputs and ratios—bear little relation to the research into what constitutes educational effectiveness. Blau and

Currie find "little convincing evidence that structural child care inputs affect child outcomes."[41] Or, as Pianta explains it:

> Many states and localities measure program "quality" only in terms of proxies—the credentials of teachers, the size and spaciousness of the facilities, the amount of learning material available, and the length of the preschool day. Except for the last characteristic, these "quality indicators" do not measure what programs offer young children that is educationally important. Still, these indicators often drive program design and policy.

Pianta and his colleagues mounted an elaborate study to see whether either the ECERS benchmarks or the NIEER program standards were closely linked with the actual classroom behaviors and activities most apt to foster "academic, language and social development" among four-year-olds. The results of their investigation showed almost no relationship between those widely used standards and actual cognitive outcomes for kids. While the authors did not openly criticize the criteria of ECERS and NIEER (and, implicitly, NAEYC), indeed suggested that such criteria might help to screen programs for basic adequacy, they also found that classrooms and centers that fared well on those criteria did not necessarily boost the school readiness of their young participants.[42] (Pianta and colleagues have developed their own assessment of teacher-child interactions in the pre-K setting, particularly instructional interactions, that does predict gains in kids' outcomes.)

Why does so much of the pre-K field fuss about inputs and structures when these do not equate to program effectiveness and thus not to quality as properly defined for today's education world? Because, for one thing, inputs are far easier to measure. The human interactions that truly matter can only be gauged by placing sophisticated observers inside classrooms over long periods. This is doable—Pianta and colleagues have trained more than a thousand such observers—but it's time-consuming, relatively costly, and (unless done with care) vulnerable to charges of subjectivity and inconsistency.

Another reason is surely habit, the fact that ECERS and NAEYC were evaluating day care and preschool programs long before today's preoccupation with kindergarten readiness and gap-closing. NIEER, too, has been making waves for years now. Those organizations' measures, criteria, and emphases simply cannot bear the burden we're now asking them to carry, as if we were expecting the sanitation inspector also to appraise the nutritional value of the restaurant's cuisine. But once something gets used in certain ways and that usage becomes widespread, it attracts believers, practitioners, and habitués, and becomes harder to alter.

Yet another explanation, certainly the most troubling, is that the kinds of quality criteria for pre-K programs that Pianta and others favor typically yield glum findings precisely because so few pre-K classrooms display such attributes as high-quality interactions between skilled teachers and children. Wide application of the proper criteria would lead to many extant programs, centers, and operators being found lacking, a profoundly unwelcome message for advocates and operators.

"If one were to rest the whole system on those structural indicators that people tend to talk about," Pianta says, "you could vastly overestimate the level of quality that is in the system."[43] This can be discouraging. Pianta himself is pessimistic about large-scale implementation of high-quality programs, noting that "when these approaches are disseminated to large groups of preschool teachers through districtwide training or college courses, such approaches typically have a much-reduced effect on outcomes, often because the quality of implementation is low."

A further explanation is philosophical resistance to a cognitive view of pre-K quality. Particularly when dealing with small children, adults must certainly attend to "the whole child" and his/her varied developmental needs. Nevertheless, in today's pre-K policy context, what matters most is a program's effectiveness in imparting essential school-readiness skills to its young participants, principally in the cognitive domain. Key attributes of such programs include clear goals, accurate assessments, and a willingness to be judged by outcomes, as well as by the high-quality classroom interactions most apt to yield them. But that isn't how most early-childhood educators prefer to view their work, much less to be evaluated on their performance.

This is a field, like so much of American education, whose culture and belief structure have long been profoundly "child-centered," "nurturing," and pedagogically progressive, in love with wild flowers and repelled by crop cultivation. E.D. Hirsch depicts this "thought-world" in his important book, *The Schools We Need and Why We Don't Have Them:*

> From Romanticism, the American educational community inherited the faith that early childhood is a time of innocence and naturalness, a time for *being* a child....It is wrong to spoil the one time of life when children can develop in tune with the order of things....Self-evidently, premature book learning goes against nature. According to the educational community, "research has shown" that untimely interventions and constraints are "developmentally inappropriate" and create a hothouse, forced-feeding atmosphere....Such expert attacks against early book learning intensify the already powerful Romanticism in American culture....[44]

Parents, too, are not of one mind in selecting preschool and day-care arrangements for their children. When asked on a recent survey what factors were "very important" in choosing centers for their (three-through-five-year-old) youngsters, "learning activities" were cited by 81 percent. But 88 percent emphasized "reliability," 73 percent looked for "time with other children," and 60 percent were concerned with "location." (Interestingly, just 37 percent deemed cost "very important," though that rose to 53 percent among parents below the federal poverty line.)[45]

In the early childhood years in particular, family priorities differ greatly, and particularly because nothing at this age is compulsory, a complex and messy system has arisen that caters to varied tastes and needs. It's hard to imagine homogenizing such a system—and far from clear that doing so would make sense from a policy standpoint or prove politically acceptable.

What changed over the past quarter century in the compulsory domain of K–12 education was that "outside" reformers—governors, business leaders, even Congress—insisted that schools prove themselves successful according to how much their pupils learn in relation to pre-set standards and learning objectives. That is by no means a flawless strategy and I have often faulted the standards-based reform effort in primary-secondary education for its shortcomings.[46] But in time we'll get it close to right, and external accountability for demonstrated results will remain the name of the K–12 game.

Nobody would want a young child's readiness for kindergarten to be gauged solely in terms of cognitive achievement. Dressing oneself, standing in line, sharing toys, and gaining control over large and small bodily movements are crucial, too, and we know from the NCLB experience the distortions that arise when too much accountability is tied to narrow measures of performance. But today's pre-K world remains a long way from having to worry about that dilemma. Its current problem in gauging program quality is not just its disinclination to judge children's school readiness but also its aversion to judging programs by their results (however defined and measured) or even by their diligent use of practices that are known to foster good results. It's pre-Coleman, indeed.

# Murky Evidence

Given the shaky, antiquated condition of standards and judgments of quality in this field, we ought not be surprised that the evidence to date about what works and what lasts is confused and ambiguous. Countless studies of dozens of programs of many sorts have yielded findings and conclusions that point in every direction. Indeed, preschooling painfully illustrates the discouraging epigram about education research (and much else in social science): if you tell me what conclusions you'd like, I can point you to a study that meets your needs. This circumstance alone should caution readers against succumbing quickly to anything that claims to be a consensus of research in this field. Discord reigns.

That being so, is there anything useful to be gleaned from prior investigations into what pre-K education does or doesn't do, for which children, and under what circumstances? If an approach isn't effective in advancing some important public mission, after all, why have more of it at public expense? There are lots of kids out there; pre-K programs are relatively expensive; society has many needs; the economy is foundering; this policy arena is contentious; and despite all the uplifting rhetoric, zealous advocacy, and heartstring tugging on behalf of small children, taxpayers might better devote their resources to other purposes unless this one is unequivocally beneficial.

In examining the question of what works and what lasts, it's useful to note that while a number of studies find desirable short-term effects from various programs and interventions, especially for disadvantaged youngsters, few can point to significant effects that endure over time and fewer still to lasting gap reductions.

As Bruce Fuller says in summarizing the findings of numerous studies with regard to the initial impact of pre-K education:

> The short-term effects of preschooling…on poor children's cognitive growth are well established….The general effect size— even for poor children—ranges from one-fifth to one-third of a standard deviation….Significant benefits [also] accrue to children from middle-class households, but at considerably lower levels of magnitude.[47]

Fuller also notes that some studies have found a downside to placing young children in center-based care for prolonged periods. In particular, their social development may be retarded and their propensity to "act out" may rise slightly. In short, any cognitive gains may be partially offset by other losses.

On the other hand, summarizing a wide body of evidence, David Figlio finds that preschool has beneficial behavioral effects on children from the most disadvantaged circumstances, leading to "reduced student disciplinary problems and reduced rates of being classified [as] emotionally disabled or severely emotionally disturbed." These benefits, however, like the cognitive gains from preschool, are "concentrated in the least advantaged communities"; Figlio and his colleague "do not find evidence that public pre-kindergarten programs have appreciable behavioral benefits" in "relatively advantaged neighborhoods."[48]

But the big issue with pre-K education is whether the gains and gap reductions last—and for how long and in what ways. Evidence is limited because the longitudinal studies needed to answer such questions are costly, complex, and obviously time consuming. But insofar as any central tendency can be found in the research done so far, the news isn't good. Most of the gains that can be found upon entry into school ebb over time, and the differences attributable to various kinds of programs tend to wash out, too. In fact, effects that may appear significant at the conclusion of the program itself frequently fade to the vanishing point. Because that erosion is at least as much a commentary on the public schools (and children's lives outside school) as on early-education programs per se, it also underscores the folly of making pre-K policy in isolation.

Let me illustrate with an example from *kindergarten* research, addressing a basic question: the relative merits of full- versus half-day programs for children from varying circumstances. In 2001, three-fifths of U.S. kindergartners were in full-day programs, and in many states a vigorous argument asserts that *all* programs should be full-day. That has become its own hot policy (and budgetary) issue, akin to expanding pre-K programs. The RAND Corporation finds that, while full-day programs yield greater achievement gains during the kindergarten year itself, by the end of third grade no significant differences are detectable in academic performance. In fact, most of the effect has vanished by the completion of first grade.[49] That's because the school experience swamps the kindergarten effect—and is in turn overwhelmed by the "risk factors" (race, poverty, family, etc.) that some children bring with them to school.

We ought not be too surprised. After all, a typical one-year kindergarten (or pre-K) program, even a relatively ambitious one that operates six hours per day for some 200 days, will affect a child for just 1,200 of the 8,760 hours in his/her life that year, never mind the tens of thousands of hours that precede and follow the pre-K experience. For poor and middle-class youngsters alike, albeit in very different ways, the impact of the program is trumped by the many other forces at work in their lives. A child's "fade" could be the consequence of inferior teaching in the early grades, the delayed effect of weak vocabulary and a meager knowledge base that persist in school even when certain "pre-literacy" skills like "decoding" are present at the onset of kindergarten, or other causes barely understood.

Compounding this problem is the fact that, just as early-education's initial impact isn't the same for all kids, its fade rate differs as well. After reviewing the pertinent research, Fuller concludes that, "for children from middle-class and affluent families, few sustained benefits from preschool have been observed," a finding echoed by Figlio's analysis of the behavioral impact of preschooling.[50]

We must also face the fact that children aren't all the same, even when they hail from similar backgrounds. Anyone who has spent time around little kids knows that, despite identical stimuli and nurturing, they develop various competencies at different stages. Some, for example, master the motor skill of "coloring within the lines" before entering kindergarten, while others are still scribble-scrabbling in first grade. That difference doesn't necessarily reflect the teaching they did or didn't receive.

Yet the policy dilemma is inescapable: how important is it to expand participation in programs and services whose effects are unpredictable and uneven or that don't last? It's a fine thing to give kids an early boost along life's highway. But how high a priority can this be when, not far down that road, either those kids slow down or others pick up speed (or both) and the pre-K advantage slowly ebbs?

As Fuller notes, "How to sustain the initial benefits of preschool is turning out to be a pivotal question. Even if [programmatic] quality gains yield modest improvements in children's trajectories, a bump of one-fifth to one-fourth of a standard deviation initially isn't likely to persist very far into elementary school. It will be swamped by the disparate effects of children's home environments, which often mirror the quality of elementary schools entered."[51]

Yes, there's some evidence, much debated, that ultra-intensive pre-K programs have greater and longer-lasting effects. But fasten your seat belt, because the programs that everyone cites in this regard—notably Michigan's Perry Preschool and North Carolina's Abecedarian Project—turn out to be truly exceptional. They were richly financed, highly sophisticated, multifaceted interventions in the lives of extremely disadvantaged youngsters and their families—and they took place decades ago. Fuller calls them "boutique programs." Besharov favors the term "hothouse programs," noting that they were "run by top-notch specialists,...served fewer than 200 children, cost at least $15,000 per child per year in today's dollars, often involved multiple years of services, had well-trained teachers, and instructed parents on effective child-rearing. Significantly, the children they served had low IQs or had parents with low IQs."[52]

Some studies have found that these programs had positive impacts on their participants that endured into adulthood, such as reducing their likelihood of incarceration. That's obviously encouraging, albeit rather remote from the school readiness and academic gap-closing that are customarily proffered as reasons for more and better pre-K education. But the two programs' long-term effects also turned out to be uneven and mostly small. In a 2005 appraisal, when the original Perry Preschool participants were turning forty, analysts reported that (in Fuller's words):

exposure to Perry explains less than 3 percent of all the variation in earnings...and about 4 percent of the variability in school
attainment levels....Reduction in the total number of criminal
arrests was significant in some years and not for others; at age
forty it was significant for males, but not for females. In short,
findings for some key outcomes are inconsistent across years, and
alleged benefits reported in the popular media fade out in terms
of statistical significance.[53]

Similarly mixed conclusions about long-term effects apply to the
Abecedarian Project, which delivered exceptionally intensive birth-
to-kindergarten services—some thirteen times as many "preschool
intervention service" hours per child as Head Start provides—to
a small number of low-income black children in North Carolina
between 1972 and 1977. On the plus side, Besharov and his colleagues agree, the program "achieved positive and lasting gains on a
wide range of cognitive and school-related outcomes, including IQ,
reading, and mathematics achievement scores." On the other hand,
"these gains became ambiguous as time went on" and "did not lead
to many improved outcomes in adulthood...with, for example, no
statistically significant differences in high school graduation rates,
employment, or criminal activity."[54]

After a sophisticated re-analysis of both the Perry and Abecedarian
results, Berkeley economist Michael Anderson found "positive, significant overall long-term effects on females" but practically no lasting positive effects for males. (A somewhat similar program in Tennessee that
Anderson examined yielded few results for either girls or boys.)[55]

Also widely admired and much discussed in the field is the
Chicago Child-Parent Center, which has operated for four decades
under the aegis of that city's public school system with funding
from the federal Title I program. (Annual cost per preschooler:

about $5,400.) Its primary evaluator, the University of Wisconsin's Arthur J. Reynolds, reports positive and lasting effects from the center's efforts, though Besharov raises methodological issues with the studies and finds the "effect sizes" reported by Reynolds to be no more than modest.

Except perhaps in the case of Chicago, it's doubtful that the conditions, circumstances, and cost structures of these boutique programs are readily replicable on a large scale. Neither Perry nor Abecedarian has yet been successfully reproduced in ways that allow independent analysts to determine whether the program's effects were also reproduced. And it's naïve to suppose that these programs' intensive features would be found in the sort of universal program that pre-K advocates are bent on creating. (Perry Preschool cost about $17,000 per participant per year; Abecedarian served children for five years at a total cost per participant of about $74,000. Both figures are in 2005 dollars.) Ironically, advocates' success in pushing for more universal-style pre-K programs is probably dimming the prospects for more Perry-style intensive interventions in the lives of the neediest children and families.

The acclaimed hothouse programs also had many moving parts, and no one can say for sure which (if any) of them mattered more than others. Abecedarian, for example, ran year-round from infancy to kindergarten entry, afforded each child an individualized education plan, and provided parents and families with sundry added services. To the extent that it had a lasting impact, nobody knows which elements were most consequential and therefore which are most important to try to incorporate into large-scale successor programs. Policymakers and taxpayers therefore face considerable risk of locking into huge new programs a costly array of services and activities that may or may not contribute materially to the desired education results.

There's also a problem in using long-term outcomes from Perry Preschool et al. in such spheres as adult incarceration to argue for (and against) contemporary pre-K programs. It borders on the absurd to expect preschool experiences, however robust, to ameliorate all of life's challenges and problems far into the future. I for one would be satisfied with evidence that a year or two of preschool could reduce achievement gaps to near-invisibility upon entry into kindergarten provided that the K–12 system then devised methods for keeping the gaps from re-opening in the elementary grades.

Yet the separate and self-referential policy universe of pre-K education deepens the challenge of maintaining preschool gains after children enter "regular school." Their fade-out in K–12 is plainly not a problem that pre-K policy alone can solve or should be expected to solve. Moreover, the pre-K world's only real way of addressing it—redoubling and intensifying its own programs, a la Perry and Abecedarian—exceeds what a large-scale venture could reasonably contemplate.

Sustaining whatever pre-K gains can be produced, especially for poor kids, is therefore principally a challenge for K–12 policy and practice. But that challenge becomes no easier when pre-K education is entrusted to public-school systems. Today, those systems cannot even sustain their own gains—which is why American fourth graders tend to have stronger results than eighth graders and high school students do less well than middle schoolers. Adding more years to the present K–12 mandate of public education would, I fear, simply give ineffectual school systems additional time to fumble around while entangling pre-K education more tightly in the webs of public-school politics, federalism disputes, bureaucratic rigidities, and adult interest groups.

Why preschool gains dissipate and gaps don't stay narrowed has much to do with unchanging home and neighborhood situations. But we must also ruefully acknowledge, despite all the K–12 education reforming of recent decades, the crummy, ineffectual schools that most poor children still enter, the absence of decent choices among schools, and the system's still-widespread weak expectations, limp curricula, slipshod accountability, and ill-prepared, ill-compensated, ill-motivated, and often inexperienced teachers.[56]

Besides all that, kindergarten and primary-grade teachers tend to "batch-process" their pupils, so that youngsters arriving with skills and knowledge already acquired in preschool must tread water, educationally speaking, while their instructors struggle to ready those who entered without that earlier boost.[57] Despite much talk of individualized learning, few teachers—especially those most apt to be found in inner-city schools—are truly able to differentiate their instruction according to whether a given child did or didn't bring certain knowledge and skills with him/her. The lowest common denominator among a classroom's pupils is apt to become the level of instruction for everybody.[58]

On the bright side of the continuity divide between pre-K and K–12 education, we observe growing interest among policymakers in developing an education system that seamlessly advances and tracks young people from preschool through college (and sometimes beyond), with synchronous standards, multiple options, and robust data systems, all helping to ensure that individuals don't "fall through the cracks" and that policymakers can get better information about how the system is working and what needs attention. Thus some states are developing "P-16 councils" and the like, intended to harmonize and align their education offerings from early childhood into adulthood. And despite pushback from "privacy" advocates, most states are developing "unique student identifiers" and other ways of monitoring the progress of individual youngsters as they pass through the various levels of the system and move from school to school and town to town. The interstate mobility problem remains to be tackled, however. So, unfortunately, does the development of effective links between the K–12 and pre-K data systems.

# The Florida Story

Unlike most of the Sunshine State's wide-ranging education reforms of the past decade, Florida's voluntary pre-kindergarten program (VPK) was not an initiative of Governor Jeb Bush. It resulted from a constitutional amendment, overwhelmingly passed by voters in November 2002. Preschool activists and citizen reformers campaigned hard for the amendment, convinced that Floridians needed and wanted a universal pre-K program but that the legislature, left to its own devices, wasn't likely to give them one.

The ambitiously worded mandate says that:

Every four-year-old child in Florida shall be provided by the state a high quality pre-kindergarten learning opportunity in the form of an early childhood development and education program which shall be voluntary, high quality, free, and delivered according to professionally accepted standards. An early childhood development and education program means an organized program designed to address and enhance each child's ability to make age appropriate progress in an appropriate range of settings in the development of language and cognitive capabilities and emotional, social, regulatory and moral capacities through education in basic skills and such other skills as the Legislature may determine to be appropriate.

The governor and legislature had to determine exactly what all those words meant and how to translate them into action. After a false start or two, they decided that VPK operations would be entrusted to the state's Agency for Workforce Innovation, a "manpower" department charged primarily with welfare-to-work programs but also responsible for coordinating county-level "early learning coalitions"—quasi-governmental bodies that were already charged with local oversight of the state's existing preschool and child-care programs.

The 94-page statute they enacted in 2005 included ten key elements:

+ Universal but voluntary. Florida's pre-K program is not means tested; lawmakers understood that it would yield a tax-financed windfall for some participants. It's voluntary and available to every four-year-old residing in the state (no citizenship requirement). It's also free: no registration fees, materials charges, etc., though parents are responsible for transportation and ancillary costs.

+ Families are supposed to have ample choices among multiple preschool providers of every sort: public and private, for- and nonprofit, secular and "faith based."

+ A basic program of 540 hours is provided during the school year (often but not necessarily translated as three hours a day for 180 days). That might be a youngster's entire pre-K experience or, for families seeking a longer program, might be enveloped by other governmental or parent-paid child-care and school-readiness offerings. (Providers may charge what they like for the "wraparound" activities but must accept VPK's $2,677 per child—the 2007-08 figure—as full payment for the core program.)

+ Alternatively, for parents preferring it, a summer-before-kindergarten program totaling three hundred hours must be offered by all public-school systems, and may also be delivered by qualified private providers.

+ After much negotiation with private operators that wanted no such constraints, lawmakers placed input-type limits on staff-child ratios and class sizes. They also mandated the licensing of teachers and staff. Summer-program teachers (predominantly in public schools) must have college degrees or be certified. School-year teachers must have a state-issued (or national) Child Development Associate certificate; they need not be college graduates but must complete an "emergent literacy" (reading readiness) course approved by the Department of Education.

+ In Tallahassee, an agency troika is in charge. The Education Department sets program standards, provides professional development to staff and oversees the accountability system; the Department of Children and Families licenses providers and staffers; and the Agency for Workforce Innovation and its local coalitions handle day-to-day administration.

+ The county-level coalitions' boards were reorganized to bestow leadership on governor-appointed businesspeople rather than early-childhood stakeholders.

+ VPK is avowedly a pre-kindergarten program, not a child care service. Its state-prescribed education standards span seven domains, including health and social/emotional/motor development as well as "language and communication," "emergent literacy," and "cognitive development and general knowledge." Now in the process of updating those standards as part of a three-year cycle,[59] revisers intend to do for the math-readiness portions of the standards (and accompanying assessments) what the initial round did for reading readiness.[60]

+ Besides providing emergent-literacy courses for pre-K instructors, the Education Department offers professional development programs, publications, and online options to teachers and administrators, as well as guides for parents.

+ The VPK program strives to be results based, with a relatively light regulatory touch when it comes to most inputs and services. Providers may, for example, use whatever curriculum they like. The key test of VPK's effectiveness is assessment of the kindergarten readiness of the children involved.

Unlike Oklahoma, Georgia, and other states, it was never expected that Florida's pre-K program would be run by the public schools. A wide array of private child-care and preschool operators, most of them for-profit, were to be the chief providers. Faith-based programs were welcome. So were school systems if they had the capacity and inclination. Their only obligation, however, was to operate a summertime version.

Florida has some 220,000 four-year-olds, and nobody knew how many families might take advantage of the new pre-K option. Thousands were already involved with other public pre-K programs, plus "private pay" preschools, formal and informal child care, and all the rest. Nor was anyone sure in advance how many—and which kinds—of the state's multitude of preschool operators would want to participate in VPK. Some already had plenty of clients, and the new program brought uncertain enrollments, added regulation, modest funding, and new worries. (Would it still exist in five years? Would its meager per-pupil budget be slashed? Would school systems gobble it up? Would faith-based efforts retain their religious integrity?)

Florida mounted a universal program with impressive speed. In year two (2006-07), VPK already served 126,000 youngsters, about 55 percent of the eligible age cohort, and was headed toward 60. That doesn't mean only three-fifths of Florida's four-year-olds take part in pre-K programs, since thousands more still enroll privately or under other publicly-financed arrangements in a host of other schools, centers, and in-home arrangements. It does mean, however, that the state is intentionally supplying a purposeful pre-K education program, with cognitive standards, assessments, and accountability mechanisms built in, to a very large number of children.

Of the 5,000-plus VPK providers in 2006-07, 19 percent were public schools (predominantly operating summer programs), and nearly all the rest were private operators. (Small numbers of children were served by "family child care centers," typically in a private home.)

It's relatively easy to become a VPK provider, but in order to remain in the program, successful results are supposed to follow. Although lobbying by the child-care industry led to relatively gentle performance requirements, chronic non-performers are meant to be "counseled out" of the program or dropped from it. Pre-K advocates fault the state for not imposing more up-front rules on VPK operators, especially in the realm of staff credentials. Florida opted instead for a standards and results-based program, much as it has done in the K–12 sphere. Its VPK education standards are ambitious, particularly in the cognitive domain.[61] (This is one area in which the otherwise-critical NIEER gives top marks to the Florida program.) They are intentionally aligned with the state's primary-grade standards, and an effort is underway to align the student assessments, too.[62] The goal is to ensure that VPK graduates are truly ready to succeed in kindergarten.

At present, assessment of kindergarten readiness occurs through a trio of measures that enable the state to compare children who

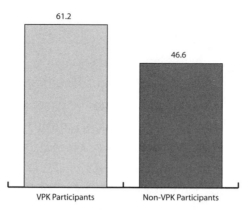

**FIGURE 3** Percentage of Entering Florida Kindergartners Found Ready on All Three Measures, 2006–07

*Source:* Florida Legislature, OPPAGA report 08-23

completed the VPK program with others.[63] The early results are encouraging. (See Figure 3.) Overall, concludes the legislature's Office of Program Policy Analysis and Government Accountability, 61 percent of VPK graduates (from 2006-07) were "kindergarten ready" by all three measures, compared with 47 percent of nonparticipants. (The 2007-08 data are very similar.)[64]

These results are also tracked back to individual program operators to determine how well or poorly they prepared their young charges. Chronic low performers (defined as three consecutive years of weak results) are supposed to lose their eligibility. The legislation is timid in this regard, however: it bars the state board of education from designating more than 15 percent of all providers as low performers in a given year, and it allows providers to cycle in and out of the program as long as they don't rack up three *consecutive* years in that bottom group. Statehouse observers understand that these constraints on the accountability system stem from successful lobbying by the state's well-connected commercial child-care interests.

Still, the Department of Education does publicly identify VPK providers according to the performance of their graduates, and interested parents can access this information on a state website when choosing among operators and centers.[65]

The goal is to marshal the parent marketplace, local monitoring, the state's limited punitive sanctions, and technical assistance in order to achieve these worthy aims: help weak performers improve, boost the effectiveness of VPK providers in relation to the state's standards, encourage enrollment in high-performing centers, and deter chronic low performers from remaining in the program. And there's some evidence of success in that regard. For example, although 410 of 481 operators judged low-performing during 2005-06 stayed in the program the following year, only 157 of them reappeared on the hit list. By year three, only 254 of year one's lowest performers were still in the program (and 25 were known to have gone out of business).

Some pre-K advocates deplore Florida's approach, insisting that it doesn't sufficiently emphasize program quality, is too cheap and inadequately monitored, puts excessive emphasis on student results (rather than NIEER-style quality criteria), and defers overmuch to the interests of private providers. David Kirp, for example, excoriates the VPK program in these exaggerated terms:

> Most of Florida's preschool problems are neither transitory nor inadvertent. They represent deliberate judgments. The law contains no meaningful curricular standards, and because there is no oversight, the legislative requirement that the curriculum be "developmentally appropriate" is meaningless. There is no requirement, just a hope, that pre-K teachers will eventually be required to have even as much as an associate's degree. While the state has adopted strenuous-sounding standards...enforcement

is nonexistent. What's more, the legislation permits preschools to discriminate in deciding which children to enroll and which teachers to hire....The real winners are the for-profit and faith-based preschools....[T]hey got almost everything they asked for.[66]

State officials are undeterred, however. Florida Education Commissioner Eric Smith places high priority on "early learning success" and is striving to align the VPK program more precisely with the public schools' K-3 offerings in a continuous effort to build a strong foundation for children's reading and math performance. Florida seems truly to view pre-K as a school-readiness initiative—but one that doesn't belong to the school system.

# The Oklahoma Story

In marked contrast to Florida, Oklahoma's big, statewide pre-K program operates—and is funded—primarily through the public schools.

After a series of pilot projects in the 1980's and early 1990's, mainly in Tulsa, the Oklahoma legislature amended the school-finance formula in 1998 to allow districts to count participating four-year-olds as regular pupils for purposes of claiming state education dollars. (Districts can in fact "overweight" them and claim more funds per child than they get for older students.) There was no means-testing or other targeting of eligibility; all that mattered was being four years old and living in Oklahoma.

This promised to be a fiscal boon to struggling school systems, especially in rural communities that had been shedding population for decades, and it swiftly led most systems—97 percent of them by 2006, reports NIEER—to launch or expand their offerings for four-year-olds. With those offerings came demanding statewide rules governing class size, teacher certification, and, more recently, school-readiness standards and pre-K curricula that include a definitive cognitive thrust.

Like most states, Oklahoma already had numerous Head Start operators and private preschool providers, many of them faith based and church affiliated. It would have been impolitic and wasteful to set up a new, self-contained public program in competition with them.

So the state pre-K program was designed to encourage public schools to outsource their work, under contract, to those established providers, with school systems typically retaining a portion of the funds, ostensibly to cover administrative costs. This set-up also makes it easier for operators to combine other early-childhood programs, services, and dollars with the state-funded pre-K program and present families with a seamless blend of child care and preschooling.

Yet not all that much outsourcing has actually occurred. Of the 34,000 four-year-olds enrolled in Oklahoma's state-funded pre-K program in 2007, just 4,000 were served by these "collaboration" providers. The remaining 88 percent were in programs operated directly by school systems, prompting an assistant state education superintendent to say recently that "Now it's just another grade in school, except that it's voluntary."[67]

The 34,000 figure represents about 68 percent of the eligible population—a bit more than the corresponding percentages in Florida and Georgia—but doesn't mean that the other one-third of four-year-old Sooners have been ignored. Seventeen percent of them were in Head Start in 2007 and 5 percent in special-ed programs, meaning that only one in ten of these kids either had no outside-the-home arrangements or were in private programs.

It's hard to know how many Oklahoma families with four-year-olds have reaped a windfall from the new state program, which deploys public dollars to pay for programs or services akin to what the families would otherwise have obtained for themselves. Certainly the effort has had a modest upward effect on public school systems, adding about 5 percent to enrollments and a bit more than that to staffing (the pre-K program may have no more than ten children per staff member).

Program implementation has brought some conflict, too. In one camp are state and district education officials contending with

NCLB-style pressures to raise reading and math scores and thus keen to stress the pre-literacy and pre-numeracy side of early education. In the opposing camp are traditional "child development" people (along with veteran Head Start operators and staffers) who emphasize "whole child"-type programs and services.

By virtue of its universality and its $3,400 per-pupil state price tag (augmented by local and federal dollars that raise that figure to about $6,700), Oklahoma's program is obviously not tightly targeted, although two-thirds of participants in the Tulsa sample cited below qualified for reduced-price lunches. Nor is the program particularly intensive: three-fifths of participating children are in half-day versions. Thus far, however, it does seem to be having a modest salutary effect on participants.

Georgetown University's William Gormley and Deborah Phillips have twice evaluated entering kindergartners in Tulsa, first in 2001, then in 2003. The earlier study found cognitive gains among low-income and black and Hispanic youngsters who took part in the state pre-K program, but not among their white or middle-income counterparts. The later study found benefits among (Tulsa) children of all races and income levels, although the gains were larger among members of minorities and the poor. Unfortunately, no information is available on how well, if at all, those entering gains were sustained as the students proceeded through public school. As we have seen, the pattern in most such programs is a gradual fade-out of pre-K effects, usually to the vanishing point.

Will Oklahoma break that discouraging mold? It's too soon to know.

# The Problem of Head Start

Nowhere is resistance to structured, curriculum-based, standards-and-assessment-driven early education clearer than in the big, iconic, federal early-childhood program known as Head Start, a legacy of Lyndon Johnson's mid-1960s declaration of war on poverty. Though this program and its founders were surely not anti-education, today's enormous Head Start fan club insists that it be viewed as a child development program, not as preschool—and thereby illustrates the difficulty of incorporating a firm focus on school readiness into an established venture that has long had a softer and more diffuse mission (and a weak cognitive track record).

At the outset, little was made of the child development vs. preschool distinction. In a letter to Congress in February 1965, LBJ characterized his proposal as "a school readiness program for 100,000 children about to enter kindergarten."[68] A few months later, describing Project Head Start, then just a summer program, he said that "nearly half the preschool children of poverty will get a head start on their future. *These children will receive preschool training to prepare them for regular school in September.* [emphasis added] They will get medical and dental attention that they badly need, and parents will receive counseling on improving the home environment."[69]

Within a few years, however, studies began to suggest that the program was not, in fact, preparing children very well for regular school. In 1969, the Westinghouse Learning Corporation and Ohio University published the first major evaluation of Head Start and concluded that, while it did commendable things for needy children by way of socialization and health care, its cognitive impact on them was nil once they reached the primary grades.

This finding launched a four-decades-long battle over how to judge Head Start's effectiveness and whether it should even be regarded as an education program. Study after study—including comprehensive federal reviews in 1985 and 2005—showed time and again that the cognitive impacts were feeble and transitory. In response, Head Start's defenders and boosters, as well as the burgeoning and organized groups of program operators and staffers, denied ever more vociferously that it is primarily about school readiness—and maintained that it should not be appraised that way. Meanwhile, appropriations ballooned. (See Figure 4.)

In other words, evidence that Head Start was not an effective education program led to the contention that it shouldn't be viewed *as* an education program![70] As Hirsch recounts, "The health, nutrition, motivation, and self-confidence of poor children were deemed to be at least as important to their future well-being as their academic learning…."[71]

Yale psychologist Edward Zigler, often termed "the father of Head Start" (and head of the program during the Nixon administration), confirms this in his own chronicle of what he calls "America's most successful educational experiment." He acknowledges that critical reviews of Head Start's educational impact encouraged supporters of the ever-expanding program to justify it on other grounds. Here is how he recalls his own response to the first negative appraisal:

When asked about the Westinghouse report, I argued that the measures used in the report were much too narrow. Don't crucify

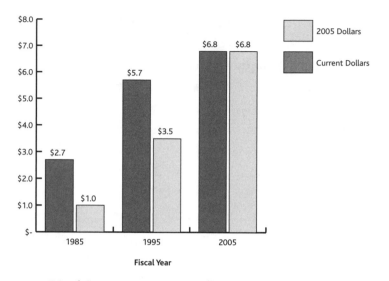

**FIGURE 4** Head Start Appropriations (billions of dollars)

*Source:* U.S. Department of Health and Human Services, Administration for Children & Families, *Head Start Impact Study*

the child on the cross of IQ, I said. Always I would repeat the theme that what we should be evaluating was not Head Start's impact on cognitive ability, but rather its influence on the motivational factors that lead children to make the most of the cognitive abilities they have. Head Start should be evaluated on much broader criteria, such as not only school performance but also health, nutrition, and attitudes toward self and society.[72]

Zigler had powerful allies, including Health, Education and Welfare (HEW) Secretary Elliot Richardson, who, he says, encouraged him to "publicize Head Start's strengths." This pattern continued for years, justifying the program on grounds of child development rather than school readiness. When the new cabinet-level education department was being stripped out of the old HEW in 1978-79, Head Start proponents campaigned fiercely and successfully to keep their program in what became known as the Department of Health and Human Services (HHS), where it remains today. They argued that it belonged with other health, welfare, and child development programs, rather than with federal education programs, as the Carter White House had proposed. Congress concurred.[73]

Contending that Head Start was only about developing, not "educating," poor children became somewhat harder to justify after *A Nation at Risk* (1983) began to re-orient America's education policy priorities from equality to quality and as schools came to be judged by their academic performance rather than their intentions. By then, however, thousands of centers across the land were employing tens of thousands of Head Start "workers," many of them poor and not well educated themselves. This was, after all, part of the War on Poverty's "community action" program, and lots of these folks came from the neighborhood. They weren't teachers in the usual sense, nor were they paid teacher-level salaries. But these jobs were important to them, their families, and their communities, and they weren't about to walk away to make room for cognitively focused preschool educators. They and their associations became a significant lobbying force, as did the operators of Head Start centers that were organized and staffed in accord with the program's child development, anti-poverty, and community-based emphases.

Conflict was inevitable. The country now yearned to boost school achievement and studies showed that under-achievement arrived with many poor children at the kindergarten door. Yet those who worked for Uncle Sam's premier pre-K program, operated its centers, and watched over it in academe and on Capitol Hill insisted that it was not and ought not be focused principally on preparing young poor children for academic success in school.

Pushed by such critics as Hirsch to reshape Head Start into something more like France's curriculum-driven preschools, Congress finally tiptoed in this direction in 1998. It ordered HHS to develop "education performance standards to ensure the school readiness of children…on completion of the Head Start program." Congress even spelled out five areas that such standards must cover, including "phonemic, print, and numeracy awareness," "increasingly complex and varied vocabulary," and "an appreciation of books." Lawmakers further stipulated that within five years, at least half of the Head Start workforce should possess associate degrees or better. (The modest goal attests to the meager credentials of the existing workforce.) And they required program operators to include child outcomes in their self-evaluations.

This reorientation did not sit well with the Head Start "community," and a further dust-up arose in 2000 when President-elect George W. Bush signaled that he intended to turn Head Start into a "reading program." Zigler harrumphed in *The New York Times* that it was *already* a reading program "at the level that is possible for children of 3 and 4." Perhaps Zigler hadn't spent much time in those French preschools that Hirsch extolled. In any case, he insisted that most Head Start-age children lack "the cognitive capacity to attribute meaning to abstract symbols, like written words. Even for the rare ones who do, most teachers agree that time is better spent learning behavior needed in school, like listening, taking turns and getting along with others."[74]

The argument about Head Start's mission flared again in 2003, when HHS Assistant Secretary Wade Horn announced that the program would begin assessing four-year-olds on their literacy, language, and math skills. The instrument would be a brief assessment that was not (despite much erroneous reporting to the contrary) a paper- and-pencil test for small children so much as a checklist that their teachers worked through with them, one by one. This exercise comprised part of the National Reporting System that was central to Horn's broader effort to boost Head Start results by gathering more robust data on cognitive outcomes and to tie the beloved federal program more tightly to the goal of school readiness—the very goal that Congress had set for it five years earlier.

Horn and his colleagues were keenly aware that plenty of evaluations had revealed Head Start's meager cognitive benefits. Indeed, 2005 brought the first findings from a massive, Congressionally-mandated "impact study" that was more faithful than its predecessors to rigorous social-science methodology (including, for example, random assignment of 5,000 three- and four-year-olds to Head Start and other kinds of community programs). Head Start participation did bring some cognitive gains, but they were small and found in just in a few domains.[75] As Besharov and Caeli Higney summarize the results:

> Head Start four-year-olds were able to name about two more letters than their non-Head Start counterparts, but they did not show any significant gains on much more important measures such as early math learning, vocabulary, oral comprehension (more indicative of later reading comprehension), motivation to learn, or social competencies, including the ability to interact with peers and teachers."[76]

Note, too, that these small gains were measured immediately upon exit from the program; there was no way to know whether they would fade as time passed. Even at the point of kindergarten entry, therefore, Head Start graduates benefited from little gap-narrowing, despite the expenditure of nearly $10,000 in federal funds on each of them. So Horn had good reason to try to beef up the program's preschool elements and to evaluate it and its providers on the basis of their cognitive outcomes. The National Head Start Association went wild, however. It feared that such assessment results would be used to appraise program operators, maybe even individual Head Start workers, and that the assessments were part of the Bush administration's grand conspiracy to turn veteran Head Start "child development aides" into teachers—maybe to replace them altogether. The program's faithful Congressional allies were swiftly drawn into the fray.

Much argument and rival testimony followed. But the program's old guard was soon winning, its familiar assumptions were being reinforced, and the wind was going out of the reformers' sails. In 2005, HHS Secretary Tommy Thompson exited. The following year, the Democrats took control of both houses of Congress. In early 2007, Horn left government, and later that year, Congress forbade continuation of the National Reporting System. Although the most recent Head Start reauthorization again pays lip service to the program's school-readiness role and its need for better-qualified staffers, no real enforcement mechanism remains or is likely to be re-established any time soon.

This Congressional aversion to true school readiness and results-based accountability for early-childhood programs, and the corresponding predilection to rely instead on staffing ratios and college degrees as proxies for program quality, extends beyond Head Start. It stretches across a host of well-meaning bills by prominent federal politicians, including former Senator and presidential candidate (now Secretary of State) Hillary Clinton. Despite its child-centered title, her "Ready to Learn" bill focused on ensuring that preschool classrooms were staffed by bachelor-degree-holding teachers. Similarly, Hawaii Congresswoman Maizie Hirono, author of the "Providing Resources Early for Kids" bill, would use associate's degrees for teacher aides as proxies for quality. And the 2008 revision of the big federal Higher Education Act, which for the first time covered early-childhood educators, again shows a total preoccupation with their formal academic credentials rather than their effectiveness in preparing children for school.

What President Obama will propose for Head Start and its ilk, besides more funding, remains to be seen.

# Costs and Benefits

On a national basis, reports NIEER, state pre-K spending per child in 2006-07 averaged $3,642, ranging from $2,379 in Arizona to more than $10,000 in New Jersey.[77] Florida operates its big, statewide VPK program for less than $3,000 per pupil, while Head Start spends almost $10,000. Today's annual price tag for yesterday's high-intensity programs such as Perry Preschool would exceed $15,000.[78] That's also roughly the tuition at upscale private preschools in New York and Washington. Programs serving babies and toddlers are costlier still, mainly because of state-mandated staffing ratios. (In Maryland, for example, day-care centers must have at least one staff member for every three children younger than 18 months.)

Plainly, there's no one price tag for pre-K education in America today. It depends entirely on the nature of the program: the location and duration (length of day and year), services and facilities, ages of the children, and, above all, size and pay scale of the staff. (It also depends on the amount of profit sought by private operators and their investors.) Indeed, the variability in prices exceeds even that of K–12 education. As Henry Levin of Columbia's Teachers College writes, "even a casual scrutiny of available expenditure data reveals an enormous variance between the most expensive and least expensive preschool provisions."[79]

Discussions of pre-K costs are complicated, too. Levin notes that they "are borne by many sources and not just the government. In addition, standard government and child care center accounting systems are designed to account for *expenditures* rather than *costs*." And some costs are hidden, thanks to subsidies by churches and charities, volunteer staff, in-kind contributions of people's homes or club facilities, and other entities and people.

For the sake of simplicity, however, consider that the United States has almost four million four-year-olds. A truly universal program—one that actually served all of them—would cost not less than $11.6 billion a year at the low-budget Florida end and as much as $57.8 billion at the high-budget Perry Preschool end. Including three-year olds would at least double those sums.

If we assume universal participation and pick a cost mid-point— say, $9,000 per child, which is close to where Head Start is today and approximates average per-pupil spending on K–12 public education—the outlay for four-year olds would be about $36 billion per annum. Serving three-year-olds, too, would at least double that figure, and adding the birth-to-age-three cohort would swell it to nearly $200 billion.[80]

Some believe that's a bargain, particularly when set alongside, say, the Pentagon budget or the cost of a Wall Street "bailout." But we must keep even $36 billion in perspective. That roughly equals the entire (pre-stimulus) K–12 appropriation of the Department of Education, is close to five times the current Head Start appropriation as well as ten to twelve times what states have been spending on pre-K education, and is more than triple the campaign pledge that Barack Obama made in this area.

More troubling, at least to parsimonious taxpayers who prefer to avoid paying for avoidable windfalls, is this calculation: if 85 percent of four-year-olds already participate in some sort of pre-K program, as much as $30 billion of that $36 billion figure would replace money that is presently being spent by someone—federal or state programs, private charity, and out-of-pocket by parents— while as little as $6 billion would go to pre-K services for children who currently have none—provided  they participate. Since no pre-K program will be compulsory, at least some of the families that don't sign on today will not do so tomorrow, either because they're too disorganized or because they truly don't want it for their kids.

To be sure, non-participation would reduce the price tag, and some offsetting savings would result from offsetting scale-backs of other programs and services. But it would be wrong to think of the cost as a wash. Many of the existing programs and services would still be needed for child-care purposes; even Perry Preschool tended its participants less then three hours a day. The financial relief bestowed on millions of families that currently pay out of pocket would not flow back to government; neither, obviously, would the windfall to parents who currently pay nothing for child care but instead rely on the free services of family members, friends, neighbors, churches, and others. For them, one might say, the state would begin to hire staff to do for Junior and Sis what Grandma presently does gratis. (We may wonder if the paid staff will be as attentive, affectionate, and adaptable as Grandma, or as apt to read stories, take walks, and converse.) Because universal programs are by definition not means-tested, the windfall effect would include the families of professors, neurosurgeons, and trust-fund beneficiaries as well as waitresses, bus drivers and migrant workers.

The other side of pre-K economics is the gnarly business of trying to calculate cost-benefit relationships. As in most education studies, some of the benefit from a preschool program or other intervention accrues to individual participants. They may be happier and less apt to drop out of school later; they may earn more money and/or not wind up in jail. Other possible benefits, however, flow to society in general, which may reduce the need for remedial programs in school and college as well as for the maintenance of people on welfare, in prison, etc.

How to sort that out, and especially over what period of time to calculate it, adds up to an analytic nightmare. Is it right to count the costs of a one- or two-year, part-time program against the putative private and societal benefits over half a century? How reasonable is it to attribute, let's say, a positive earnings differential at age forty to a preschool program that one took part in at age four?

The most dramatic claims for "investing in young children" have been made by economist James Heckman, who argues that this is a fundamentally important national strategy for building human capital, enhancing workforce productivity, and reducing welfare-type outlays. His analyses have been widely cited by pre-K advocates and, we read, taken seriously by President Obama (presumably not just because they're both from Chicago). It's crucial to note, however, that Heckman actually confines himself to *disadvantaged* children—not the full range embraced by universal pre-K programs—and that the evidence he cites is based on analyses from the "hothouse" Perry Preschool, Abecedarian, and Chicago Parent-Child Center programs. Although this may strengthen the case for highly targeted, high-intensity intervention programs for severely disadvantaged preschoolers, it does little to advance the "universal" argument.

On the grounds of economic returns, in fact, Heckman plainly states that his analysis has led him to favor funding for targeted pre-K programs for disadvantaged youngsters, not those that enroll everyone. Writing in the *Wall Street Journal* in 2006, he acknowledged that, because "Children from advantaged environments received substantial early investment" from their families, "there is little basis for providing universal programs at zero cost." Doing the latter would be inefficient, costly, wasteful of public dollars, and probably not effective in helping poor kids.[81]

This clarification by Heckman proved awkward for such partisans of the universal approach as Kirp, Zigler, and NIEER's Steve Barnett, who have since sought out less eminent economists to buttress their case and turned to different kinds of arguments on behalf of universality (e.g., the evils of "segregating" poor kids).

Bruce Fuller dismisses attempts to generalize from boutique efforts like Perry Preschool when deriving cost-benefit estimates for universal pre-K programs. He compares that to "looking at the cognitive acumen or earnings of Harvard graduates, and then using this rate of return to justify building more community colleges."[82]

It also stands to reason that the broader the population served, the smaller the effects and returns one will detect, at least through conventional evaluations. But in this regard, there *is* evidence that targeted or means-tested programs are more effective than universal programs. After a careful review of numerous cost-benefit studies, the University of Wisconsin's John Witte concluded that pre-K "programs that are targeted at 200 percent of the poverty line or less have more than double the rate of return of universal programs."[83]

Clive Belfield of Queens College (CUNY) struggled to estimate the costs and benefits of a universal program in New York by trying to calculate the later savings to the state's K–12 system resulting from pupils who have been through preschool. He asserts that these youngsters are less apt to repeat grades, less likely to be routed into special education, and generally prone to be "more productive" as learners. Inevitably, though, much of his evidence is also drawn from targeted programs like Perry rather than broad-based endeavors. After making innumerable assumptions and analytic leaps, he concludes that, for New York State, the medium-term cost savings from a universal pre-K program would offset between 41 percent and 62 percent of the total expenditures. In other words, the net cost over time of such a program would be roughly half of the initial price tag. But what does that mean in actual dollars?

According to NIEER, Georgia spent about $300 million on its pre-K program in 2006-07. Belfield's analysis—if correct and generalizable to other states—would suggest that the true cost to Georgia (after later education savings are factored in) was closer to $150 million.[84] Of course, state budget directors and legislators—not to mention taxpayers—are more likely to worry whether they can afford a program for which they must write checks today.[85]

# Rival Delivery Systems

As in K–12 and higher ed, pre-K education today is a mishmash of public and private institutions as well as government mandates and individual choices. As pre-K expands, however, policymakers must thread their way among three alternative (though overlapping) approaches to its delivery, each with advocates and critics as well as reasonably clear pluses and minuses.

First, pre-K can operate as a government program using public-sector providers, typically local school systems. That's the Oklahoma approach and the preference of many advocates. Libby Doggett, the kinetic head of Pre-K Now, told Fuller that "We want to build [universal pre-K] as part of the system, to professionalize the field."[86] Gene Maeroff seems to take for granted that schools should operate pre-kindergartens for all kids as an automatic adjunct to their kindergartens. And that's the version predictably favored by some potent public-school interest groups. Since 2003, for example, the National Education Association's goal in this realm has been "access for all three- and four-year-old children to a full-day *public school* pre-kindergarten of the highest possible quality, universally offered, and funded with public money not taken from any other education program [emphasis added]."[87] (Other public-school groups, such as the Council of Chief State School Officers, say they'd be content with multiple public and private providers so long as access is universal and instruction of high quality.)[88]

Second, pre-K services can be delivered through a range of operators with which the government contracts or to which it makes grants for this purpose. These typically include school systems and may also include private (for- and nonprofit) preschool providers. Georgia and several other states follow this approach, as does the federal Head Start program, which deploys some 1,600 separate grants for this purpose. Parents choose among centers; but the breadth of their options depends on how many operators the state engages in a given geographic area.

Although several studies suggest that most Georgia program participants are in privately operated centers, I made a casual check (via the state program's website) of approved pre-K providers in the Atlanta zip code where my baby granddaughter lives; I found just three such operators, two of them public elementary schools, the third a nonprofit center specializing in children with disabilities. Then I checked rural Sumter County (home of Jimmy Carter) and found that there the only state-funded pre-K options are located in public elementary schools; however, private alternatives abound if one simply Googles "preschool" in Sumter County.

Third, government can give parents vouchers and encourage them to deploy these resources at whatever pre-K facilities suit them. The choice is never completely wide open because of state licensing requirements and regulations on centers that seek pre-K education dollars. No state presently runs a major pre-K program on a pure voucher basis, but the federal Child Care and Development Fund—a legacy of the 1996 welfare-reform act—distributes billions annually in this fashion. In 2005, 89 percent of the 1.75 million youngsters whose parents were aided by CCDF subsidies had their care funded through vouchers (or cash) rather than state-contracted provider services. This is a huge program—close to $10 billion in fiscal 2006, thrice what NIEER says all 50 states spend on pre-K education—and about three-fifths of the kids benefiting from it are served in center-based programs rather than in private homes.[89] Yet many states have waiting lists for CCDF subsidies, as more families seek (and qualify for) this form of assistance than can at present receive it.[90]

Those who have studied CCDF find virtues in its use of vouchers. After looking closely at nine states, Mathematica Policy Research's Gretchen Kirby and Andrew Burwick concluded in 2007 that "Vouchers are well-suited to the delivery of child care subsidies, because their flexible and portable nature allows families to freely access the arrangements best matched to their preferences and needs. This is particularly important because there are many factors that can play into a parent's selection of a child care arrangement.... [V]ouchers can contribute directly to increasing client choice by expanding the network of providers...."[91]

John Witte, known for his doubts about the worth of primary-secondary vouchers in Milwaukee, nonetheless urges a voucher delivery system for the means-tested pre-K program he recommends for states. Considering pros and cons, he comes down in favor of vouchers because they have (a) proved popular with parents; (b) expanded access to child care while drawing a wider array of providers and services to the field; (c) put low-income families within striking distance of relatively expensive programs; and (d) thus far not been challenged in court as unconstitutional (though they may yet be, particularly in states with "Blaine amendments"). In addition, Witte says, vouchers trigger market pressures that yield greater efficiencies and economies of delivery.[92]

Even liberal sociologist Bruce Fuller sees merit in vouchers, noting that "consolidating the over $18 billion in [current] public support [for the various forms of care] into one stream of funding to preschool organizations and a single voucher program, and then decentralizing management to local counties, could lead to an easier-to-access, higher-quality network of organizations and caregivers."[93]

But vouchers bring complications, too. Besides the possibility of judicial challenge, state licensure and regulation constrain the number and variety of providers. Voucher amounts determine how many operators will fall within a family's economic reach.[94] If per-child sums are too meager or participation regulations too burdensome, not enough (or not the right sorts of) providers will participate. Not all families are skilled at selecting thoughtfully from their available options. Appropriations limits—CCDF is not a true entitlement program—make for lengthy waiting lists, even for eligible families. In addition, income limits—many states cap CCDF eligibility at 85 percent of median income—may punish parents who are fortunate enough to get a promotion or pay raise by terminating their voucher eligibility.

Vouchers place confidence in families rather than experts to know what's best for children. This does not sit well with many experts and public educators. The major pre-K advocacy groups worship at the triple altar of public financing, universality, and high quality. They typically pay lip service to the continued existence of private preschool providers, and some may be sincere in doing so. Yet the kind of system that a centralized, universal, publicly financed program usually produces tends to diminish parent choice and clamp a much-tighter regulatory regimen on providers. That's particularly true if input-style quality criteria are also superimposed and even truer when the funding stream runs—Oklahoma style—through public school systems. The reason at least 70 percent of youngsters served by state-financed pre-K programs are presently enrolled in public schools is not because they do a better job or produce stronger results but because the state programs are structured in ways that favor such providers and discourage private operators.[95]

Fuller finds multiple flaws in what he terms the standardizing approach to preschool, particularly when that means vesting responsibility in the public school system. He considers the approach dehumanizing, alienating, even undemocratic, not to mention heedless of important differences among children, families, and communities.[96]

I return to Bill Bennett's crack about the fallacy of the 14-egg omelet. With a handful of inspired exceptions, today's public schools are doing a mediocre job of educating children in general and a disastrous job of educating disadvantaged kids in particular. That's why barely one-third of U.S. students attain the "proficient" level on the National Assessment of Educational Progress and why the figures for poor and minority youngsters barely escape single digits. (In 8th grade reading in 2007, for example, just 13 percent of black students, 15 percent of Hispanics, and 15 percent of low-income youngsters ranked at or above NAEP's proficient level, and 42 percent of poor kids were below even the "basic" level.) By a variety of measures, including international comparisons, our 8th graders do worse than our 4th graders.

If our public schools are so inept at boosting and sustaining the achievement of their present students, particularly the neediest among them, one must seriously ask what would be gained—other than fattening their budgets and expanding their staffs—by widening their responsibilities to include younger children. Moreover, when it comes to truly needy babies, toddlers, and preschoolers, many of the standard features of U.S. public schools—six-hour days, 180-day years, bureaucratic management, and an off-putting stance toward parents—are ill-suited to delivering the kinds of services that would most benefit these kids and appeal to their families.[97] Nor are six-hour-a-day school systems (many still with half-day kindergarten) adept at providing the before-school, after-school, and summertime day care that working parents typically need for their little ones—and that most private operators are skilled at wrapping around a core education program. Treating pre-K as "just another grade in school" strikes me as exactly the wrong way to proceed from the viewpoint of just about everyone except, perhaps, school-system administrators and union leaders. At most, it seems to me, that system should be one among multiple optional providers of pre-K education.

Yet many in the early-education community who pledge allegiance to the principle of parental choice among multiple providers are leery of the programmatic mechanisms by which diversity and choice actually function. They are especially wary of vouchers, with essentially the same reservations as the K–12 education establishment. That is, they fret about loss of control by experts such as themselves, mistrust parents and markets, and fear that what they construe as high quality will be sacrificed to market dynamics, profit motives, etc. They insist that choices can be provided to parents via the contract approach, though it appears—Besharov believes this pattern is unavoidable—that the tendency of contract-style programs in Georgia and elsewhere is to constrain options rather severely.

Still, even a constrained market seems to yield benefits for kids. A 2006 study found that "children at nonprofit and for-profit preschools [in Georgia] did display steeper developmental trajectories [than those who took part in public-school-operated programs] as shown by higher language scores and lower retention at third grade." What's more, "All preschools that operated in a more richly competitive mixed market showed higher child outcomes."[98] In other words, the public-school programs were also more effective in places where parents had choices.

Florida's VPK program has a livelier marketplace than Georgia's (or Oklahoma's): private-sector providers comprise 81 percent of it, and many school systems participate on a limited basis, either because they lack sufficient space or because they find the per-child payment level inadequate.[99] Florida is the one large exception to the tendency of state pre-K programs to limit providers. The way that state's program works, each county's "early learning coalition" may approve any number of providers as long as they are state licensed, have some form of accreditation, and are willing to play by the program's rules and funding levels. (Some conscientious private operators have concluded, however, that the VPK program's meager per-child funding—the trade-off for universality—does not enable them to employ the staff or deliver the quality they believe desirable.)

Like primary-secondary schooling, pre-K education is not likely to settle upon a single optimal delivery system that works for every state and community, much less for every family. I see that as a plus. In a field that's already so crowded with different kinds of programs and operators, has so much competition, and serves such varied family needs and divergent priorities, it would be folly to standardize too much. Policymakers should recognize that having lots of parental options is a good thing—and that they should seek to provide needy parents with augmented purchasing power rather than enlarging the public sector, expanding the purview of the public schools, and supposing, yet again, that "one best system" can be devised for everyone. If such a system makes limited sense in K–12 education, it makes far less at the pre-kindergarten level.

It needs to be said, though, that pre-K's private sector has done a poor job of self-policing with regard to the quality and efficacy of many providers, which range from effective, reliable operators—often the large-scale chains and franchise operators of day-care, preschool, and hybrid programs—down to myriad half-baked "mom and pop" enterprises that barely satisfy minimum state-licensure requirements (or function entirely under the government's radar). It also needs to be noted that in Florida the private operators' Tallahassee lobbyists did their utmost to shield them from the state's results-based account-ability system, leading to acute limits on the Education Department's ability to eject weak performers from the program. In education as in other spheres, we need to keep in mind that providing pluralism and choice, while certainly desirable, does not satisfy the public interest. Quality counts, too, and so do results.

# A Better Route to Travel

A troubling contradiction bordering on dishonesty casts a shadow over today's mighty push for universal pre-K education in America. The principal intellectual and moral argument that advocates make—and for which I have considerable sympathy—is similar to that of No Child Left Behind backers: giving needy kids a boost up the ladder of educational (and later-life) success by narrowing or eradicating the achievement gaps that now trap far too many of them on the lower rungs. Serious pursuit of that objective would entail intensive, tightly targeted, carefully structured, means-tested, educationally sophisticated, and rigorously evaluated programs offered by an array of competent providers, starting early in a child's life, perhaps even before birth, and enlisting and assisting the child's parents from day one. The neediest and likeliest recipients of such help would be very-low-income, predominantly minority, indeed predominantly African-American, babies and children of young unmarried mothers who themselves have little education. The recipients would, in fact, resemble the targets of the much-lauded Perry Preschool and Abecedarian projects.

But their numbers are not huge. The Census Bureau reports that in 2007 the United States contained approximately two million children under the age of five living in female-headed, single-parent households with incomes below 75 percent of the federal poverty line. About nine in ten of these youngsters were black.

That works out to approximately 400,000 exceptionally at-risk youngsters per age group per year—400,000 three-year-olds, 400,000 four-year-olds, etc.—which may be compared with the roughly four *million* children in each age cohort in the United States. In other words, the most seriously at-risk subset of kids is about 10 percent of the total. These are likely to be the children in greatest need of intensive educational (and other) services if they're to have a fighting chance of succeeding in school. And those services are apt to do them the most good if begun very early in their lives, perhaps even before birth, and continued into and through the school years.

Yet the programmatic and political strategy embraced by many of today's pre-K advocates is something altogether different: furnishing relatively skimpy but widespread preschool services to all four million four-year-olds (and then, of course, all four million three-year-olds), preferably under the aegis of the public schools. Either this discordant plan is a front for public school expansionism, bent on adding another grade or two to its current thirteen, and adding the staff (and union members) that would accompany such growth, or it's a cynical calculation: only by appealing to the middle-class desire for taxpayers to underwrite the routine child-care needs of working parents will any movement occur on the pre-K front— and the heck with the disadvantaged youngsters who need more than that strategy will yield.

The research evidence, such as it is, surely doesn't support a massive expansion of uniform, low-intensity programs for all four- (and maybe three-) year-olds, at least not on grounds of boosting educational achievement or narrowing learning gaps in a lasting way. The cost-benefit analyses don't support it, either. And current participation rates make clear that a sizable portion of the price tag would yield a day-care windfall for families that do not need it—perhaps no bad thing but surely no urgent education priority in a time of strapped public-sector budgets.

On balance, it appears to me, the interests of poor kids are at present being subordinated to the politics of getting something enacted. And the unabashed reasoning behind this strategy is that nothing will be done if it's only for the poor.

That's nonsense. A number of respectable scholars have systematically debunked the original assertion by Britain's Richard Titmuss, some four decades back, that "programs for the poor are poor programs." It's also obvious that America is awash in enormous, well-funded programs that target the poor. Medicaid and Pell Grants leap instantly to mind. And in the early-childhood field, of course, there is already Head Start—spending more per pupil than any universal pre-K program is likely to cost—as well as chunks of the big Title I program that pay for pre-K education.

Surely the advocates know this. They know that "programs for the poor are poor programs" is a canard. They know that the universal programs they seek are not what would do the neediest preschoolers the most good.

To be fair, some cracks have appeared in the once-doctrinaire preschool lobby, as a handful of influential partisans shift gears from insisting on universality to urging targeted, means-tested programs. That's true, for example, of Virginia Governor Timothy Kaine; faced with both budgetary challenges and mounting opposition, he openly changed his approach in summer 2007.[100] Further, key elements of California's far-flung pre-K advocacy movement, perhaps sobered by voter rejection of the Rob Reiner initiative, now talk of "expanding access" to high-quality programs, "starting with those who need it most."[101] The New America Foundation's Sara Mead, an astute and determined pre-K booster, warned in late 2008 that "if funding gets ahead of capacity to deliver high-quality programs" in this field, "policymakers and the public could ultimately lose faith in early education." In her view, therefore, the Obama administration should "ensure that any new early education investments focus on quality... and are integrated into a broader education reform agenda."[102]

Yet program quality remains hazily—or inappropriately—defined, and swift movement toward universality remains the mantra across most of this movement, a mantra still faithfully chanted by the team at deep-pocketed Pew and key co-funders, as well as at the two main national campaign-coordinating bodies, Pre-K Now and NIEER. New state-funded, federally assisted programs serving every four-year-old remain their foremost objective. And they have influential friends in Washington, including a new education secretary who asserted during his confirmation hearing that "We have to move toward that opportunity to universal access," though it wasn't clear whether he was referring to child care, pre-K education or both.

In a rational world, it would make vastly more sense, while costing the taxpayer less money, to overhaul Head Start (and pre-Head Start and Early Head Start, etc.), existing programs that are already targeted, perhaps focusing them even more tightly on the neediest kids, making them start earlier—with those pregnant, soon-to-be single moms—and last longer, and insisting that they emphasize pre-literacy, vocabulary, and other school-readiness skills. Such programs would be delivered by standards-based, outcomes-focused, rigorously assessed providers who are willing to be judged and compared on the kindergarten readiness of their graduates. Because of ample evidence that most such gains seem to fade upon entry into K–12 schools, equal attention would be paid to revamping the early and middle grades to sustain whatever advantage these youngsters bring to school.

Accomplishing all that is a worthy challenge for the United States and one that would face obstacles aplenty even if pre-K advocates were united in pursuing it. But, of course, they're not. Besides the contentiousness of pre-K standards, the flawed notions of quality in this realm, the resistance to a tight focus on the cognitive domain, and the disputes over how to assess kindergarten readiness, we must also contend with the bevy of foundation-backed groups, public-education interests, and earnest citizens that still embrace universalism.

They surely mean well for children, and they're trying to be politically astute. But they choose not to acknowledge that what may be easier to enact and fund—a relatively low-intensity program for an enormous population of children of all sorts—is not what's best for the kids who need the most help.

Let me say it again: To compensate for conversational, educational, and cognitive shortfalls at home, boys and girls from acutely deprived environments need more intensive instruction, for more years and longer hours and in greater depth from skilled (and adequately paid) educators. Their parents (mothers, really) need help, too, and so, of course, do the schools they subsequently enter. We're not very good at doing all of that today, certainly not at scale, and we have lots still to learn.

But we do know this with near certainty: what those youngsters need surpasses what any universal program is apt to supply—and amounts to more than hordes of middle-class parents want or would even tolerate for their own kids. In pedagogic terms, acutely disadvantaged kids typically benefit from a more structured, more didactic, and lengthier program than many other parents will think desirable for their inquisitive daughters and free-spirited sons.

When I asked a prominent liberal education leader why his large California-based foundation declined to support the Rob Reiner initiative, he gave cogent reasons: The program on the ballot wouldn't concentrate the help on kids in greatest need; in a state already facing acute budget challenges, it would yield a costly windfall to families that can and do take care of themselves (and those are the families that would be most apt to take part);[103] too little thought had gone into planning the mechanisms by which it would actually be delivered, particularly the requisite facilities; and the supply of available talent to staff all those preschool classrooms, being woefully insufficient for so vast a program, would gravitate to suburban centers serving "nice" kids rather than tackling the challenges of poor and minority youngsters in tough neighborhoods. The best teachers, he predicted, would end up in the preschools with the least needy kids.

He's right—and not just about California.

Universality has another problem, too: not everyone wants it. A sizable minority of families still do an acceptable job at home without any sort of outside programs or providers. They don't want to be subjected to governmental interference with their young children; and there's some evidence that turning those kids over to standardized "institutional" arrangements isn't good for the children themselves. (This is a much-debated issue in the child care world, and the research is truly conflicted.)[104]

Critics of universal pre-K programs, including Fuller on the left, Besharov in the center and the Reason Foundation's Lisa Snell and Darcy Olsen plus the Lexington Institute's Robert Holland and Don Soifer on the right, stress such programs' limited impact, the near-ubiquitous primary- and middle-grade fade-out, and the fact that many children are being adequately served at home or by today's array of program offerings and operators.[105]

In sum, the universal approach to pre-K education has six big flaws:

+ It's expensive, with much of the cost a needless subsidy to families that are already making preschool and day-care arrangements on their own and that have children who gain little by way of school readiness from the added public outlay.

+ It does not and cannot deliver the level or type of education services that are likely to do the most good for a much smaller sub-population of severely disadvantaged, predominantly minority babies, toddlers, children, and their parents (mostly mothers).

+ Large *new* programs are apt to be less beneficial and surely pricier than retooling current programs to address the educational needs of disadvantaged youngsters. That's because the overwhelming majority of those youngsters, often starting at age three, already have access to various forms of pre-K and/or day care and because their parents already receive public subsidies to offset the cost.

+ Although much is known about what transpires in effective pre-K classrooms (and what doesn't in *ineffective* ones), not nearly enough is yet understood about the optimal mix of educational and other services and policies to prepare these kids to succeed in school—including elements of the mix that must be addressed at home by parents or other family members.[106] Hence any big, new entitlement-style program may also turn out to be ill-designed for that purpose, but get "locked in" regardless. Continued experimentation with different models makes more sense.

+ Pre-K educators and their organizations and experts have arrived at no consensus about intended outcomes, standards, or measures of effectiveness. The field itself needs to solve this problem, probably under pressure from exasperated state officials and other outsiders.

+ The "fit" between pre-K and K–12 education in the U.S. is dreadful, but probably won't be improved by giving faltering school systems greater sway over the lives of poor children. Indeed, it's clear that much of the push behind universal pre-K has less to do with needy kids than with the public education establishment's craving to enlarge its market, its budget, and its mandate.

This is not a counsel of despair. I believe that well-designed and tightly targeted pre-K programs—developed by what Fuller optimistically terms a "resourceful, surgical state"—would benefit needy kids and would do so at a lower net public cost than the universal kind. Targeting is easy to do via income-testing if the political will exists.[107] The result would be less of a windfall for those who don't need it and a substantial husbanding of scarce tax resources for those who do. This would also create the possibility that preschool programs serving acutely disadvantaged children could be as intensive and comprehensive as needed to maximize their impact on school readiness. (Alternatively, this approach could yield savings that might be redirected into current child-care programs such as CCDF vouchers, all of whose recipients are poor or close to it but thousands of whom are now on waiting lists.)

If states took the $3.7 billion that NIEER says they're presently spending on universal-style pre-K programs and concentrated those dollars on the roughly one-tenth of American four-year-olds who most need intensive preschooling, they'd have more than $9,000 per child to spend—and that's current state spending spread across a national population. Add Head Start's $7 billion (fiscal 2009 appropriation, not including the one-time "stimulus" funding) and the per-child amount swells to about $27,000. That's a decent kitty, almost enough to pay for two years of Perry Preschool-style programming, even without touching the separate federal child care dollars or tapping into other current public-sector spending on needy children. Adding the $10 billion more per year envisioned by President Obama brings the total to nearly $21 billion, at which level the per-child amount exceeds $50,000, money that could pay for education services throughout all five years of an acutely-disadvantaged youngster's pre-kindergarten life.

Whether targeted or universal, statewide or local, voucher-style or contract-style, a serious pre-K program also requires a modern data system that tracks kids easily within and beyond it. As states develop longitudinal data systems for K–12 education and begin to push them upward into postsecondary education, they should extend them downward, too, so that youngsters entering a publicly financed pre-K program are integrated into the same information base, perhaps from infancy.

States (and/or private philanthropies) should also embark upon a sophisticated program of research and evaluation of current and future programs. Besides the longitudinal tracking just mentioned, it's important to learn more about which kids are and are not participating, and why. And it would be good to know which families supplement the state program with additional pre-K or child-care of various kinds and how they pay for it. What sorts of providers serve which kids? How do families select providers, and how well informed are they when making such choices? What do parents like and dislike about particular operators? A well-conceived and -executed program would also study itself to determine, for example, whether its own assessment tools are valid and what they can and cannot predict in kindergarten and beyond.

A powerful case can still be made for well-crafted experimentation and innovation in this arena. Despite all the pilot projects, studies, and evaluations, not enough is known with certainty about the essential elements of effective pre-K education and how to make those effects last. We should welcome further trials and studies. In addition, more needs to be learned about the key elements of program quality (concentrating, please, on "process" rather than "structural" items) that can be successfully replicated and brought to scale. Nobody has yet devised the perfect pre-K program, and it's likely that different approaches will work better for different kids and circumstances. It is therefore folly for states not to try diverse designs and evaluate them all—much as, three decades ago, the federal Follow Through program did.[108] Ideally, careful experimentation and program piloting, akin to what the Minnesota Early Learning Foundation has recently undertaken, would precede large-scale implementation of any one model.[109]

If such patience proves impossible in the unsettled domain of pre-K education, a state (or private funders) should set aside resources to explore variants and alternatives, including inventive retooling of the pre-K nexus with K–12 schooling. It's important to bear in mind that the private sector, more than school systems and other public agencies, is apt to possess the imagination and nimbleness to yield true innovation in this realm—another reason why pre-K funding mechanisms and rules ought not be biased against responsible private operators.

Head Start poses special problems for federal policy makers, and they've been doing a dreadful job of solving them. Setting Head Start right—turning it into an effective pre-K program for poor kids—should be addressed by a joint effort from HHS Secretary Kathleen Sebelius and Education Secretary Arne Duncan. Despite its popularity, despite the billions spent on it, and notwithstanding the decent job it does of targeting services on needy kids, today's Head Start. when viewed through the lens of pre-K education and kindergarten readiness, amounts to a wasted opportunity. So do we just throw up our hands, keep it the way it is, and launch something different alongside it? Or do we demand the makeover it sorely needs?

Recall that Head Start operators are already supposed to provide participating children and families with "educational, health, nutritional, social and other services." The 2007 reauthorization also set as a *goal* that by 2013 all staff will possess associate's degrees and half (about twice as many as today) will have bachelor's degrees; but current law contains no sanctions for operators or centers that do not attain this goal. The same statute insists that Head Start's purpose is to "promote school readiness"; but here, too, there's no way to determine how well this is being achieved and no rewards or sanctions for program operators who do a better or worse job of producing "readiness."

The sensible course of action is to recast Head Start as a bona fide preschool education program for acutely disadvantaged children. It could remain a separate, federally run enterprise, as it has been for four decades, though it would likely work better if states could merge it and its funding with their own intensive pre-K programs. If Head Start stays separate, its educational effectiveness (and other outcomes) need to be rigorously appraised, whether through a revived National Reporting System or something designed to serve similar purposes.[110]

As for the vast complex of federally subsidized child-care programs, most of them serving low-income kids so their parents can work, I believe these are best viewed as continuing sources of day care, not early education. In the child-care realm, they appear close to getting the job done. As long as vouchers empower parents to select the providers they consider best for their kids, those who want to can choose education-heavy operators. States could help by supplying the public with clear indices or reports on each child care operation, for example on the services it provides and indicators of its effectiveness. In any case, those programs already spend many billions of dollars, and millions of children already benefit from them—further reason to shun big new ventures billed as universal.

Insofar as states focus on high-quality pre-K education programs, whether targeted or universal, they would also do well to review their traditional approach to the licensing of operators and providers. A shift by state regulators from inputs and credentials to school-readiness results might do more for needy youngsters than the addition of even more programs, dollars, and capacity. Such a shift would put needed pressure on the early-childhood field to create better readiness measures and new quality criteria. It would push private and public operators alike to concentrate on cognitive effectiveness—and staff their programs accordingly—and would drive some of the weakest operators out of business.[111]

Whatever the type of pre-K program, we also need to recall that helping kids prepare to take full advantage of their education wastes time, money, energy, and political will unless the schools into which they feed are prepared to do right by them. If not, gaps that may have been reduced by age five will reopen or widen in the early and middle grades. Youngsters who have been helped to prepare for kindergarten will gradually forfeit the benefit of that boost. Indeed, it's impossible to imagine a successful pre-K strategy that is divorced from a successful K–12 reform strategy.

Many people, myself included, have already spelled out our preferred versions of the latter strategy.[112] Restating mine in detail is beyond the scope of this discussion. In sum, however, my approach to K–12 refurbishment incorporates seven key elements: (1) solid state (or national) academic standards across the curricular core; (2) well-aligned assessments and other means of appraising individual and institutional performance in relation to those standards; (3) high-quality instructional materials and knowledgeable teachers (and/or their technology-based "distance learning" equivalent); (4) effective, behavior-changing "accountability" arrangements, including both incentives and (when needed) interventions; (5) top-flight principals with wide-ranging authority to make the important decisions about what happens and who works in their schools; (6) plenty of educational choices of good quality for families, with public resources following individual kids to the schools they actually attend; and (7) enough transparency to give everyone involved ample information about schools, educators, and results.

James Heckman, too, has doubts about the value of preschool (even for poor kids) unless it is joined with K–12 schools that sustain and enhance its benefits. But he goes farther than the schoolhouse itself. The kind of societal attention to children that he now urges includes such non-governmental efforts as "the skill-building investments that families make in their children, such as reading to kids, providing encouragement with schoolwork, and setting good examples through community service and healthy lifestyle choices."[113] When those investments are made and activities conscientiously pursued, his analysis suggests, kids turn out better according to a host of measures, and they stay that way.

Which brings us, finally, to an obvious and commonsensical conclusion: major-league success for kids depends on family and community as well as government. Where families are strong and capable, less hinges on either school or preschool. Where families are weak and communities fractured, government must do more.

But preschool is only the beginning of what must be done. Treating it and its programs in isolation, and trying to make them "fit" everybody, leads to misshapen policies, spending that's wasteful on the one hand and inadequate on the other, and gains that may be made at one level only to be forfeited at the next.

Giving young children what they need and deserve is a solemn responsibility for grownups, parents, educators, and the wider society. It requires crafting responses that differ with circumstances, don't make false promises, pay greater attention to results than to intentions and inputs, don't wield a policy cleaver when a scalpel is needed, and wherever possible utilize existing vehicles rather than placing still others on the congested highway to a better future for America's children.

# Endnotes

1. A Task Force appraisal of education reform in Florida in 2006 first led me to put a cautious toe into the pre-K pool. See Chester E. Finn Jr., "Voluntary Pre-Kindergarten," in Paul E. Peterson, ed., *Reforming Education in Florida: A Study Prepared by the Koret Task Force on K–12 Education* (Stanford: Hoover Institution Press, 2006), pp. 229-44, http://media.hoover.org/documents/ktf_florida_book_229.pdf.

2. Sam Dillon, "Obama Pledge Stirs Hope in Early Education," *New York Times*, December 16, 2008.

3. Susan Dosemagen, "Chicago Schools Expand Preschool Program: More Expansion Needed," *Medill Reports: Chicago*, October 29, 2008, http://news.medill.northwestern.edu/chicago/news.aspx?id=102553.

4. The University of Maryland's Douglas Besharov has remarked that, from a state or school district point of view, pre-K education is a "cheap date" compared with K–12 schooling—and he calculates that much of its recent increase has been funded by slower growth in other forms of child care.

5. Bold Approach Task Force, "A Broader, BOLDER Approach to Education," Economic Policy Institute, www.boldapproach.org/statement.html. For a list of signers, see www.boldapproach.org/bios.html.

6. David L. Kirp, *The Sandbox Investment: The Preschool Movement and Kids-First Politics* (Cambridge, Mass.: Harvard University Press, 2007), pp. 88-89.

7. National Early Literacy Panel, *Developing Early Literacy: A Scientific Synthesis of Early Literacy Development and Implications for Intervention* (Washington, D.C.: National Institute for Literacy, 2008), p. vii.

8. David Figlio and Jeffrey Roth, "The Behavioral Consequences of Pre-Kindergarten Participation for Disadvantaged Youth," in Jonathan Gruber, ed., *An Economic Perspective on the Problems of Disadvantaged Youth* (Cambridge, Mass.:

National Bureau of Economic Research, forthcoming), p. 16, www.nber.org/chapters/c0581.pdf.

9. See, for example, David Elkind, *The Hurried Child: Growing Up Too Fast Too Soon* (Cambridge, Mass.: Perseus Publishing, 2001). Also see Elkind, "Much Too Early!" www.besthomeschooling.org/articles/david_elkind.html.

10. See, for example, these illustrative kindergarten "content standards" from California, www.cde.ca.gov/be/st/ss/documents/elacontentstnds.pdf; these from Texas, www.tea.state.tx.us/teks/grade/Kindergarten.pdf; and these from Virginia, http://141.104.22.210/go/Sols/english.html#Kindergarten.

11. William J. Bennett, Chester E. Finn Jr., and John T. E. Cribb, *The Educated Child: A Parent's Guide from Preschool through Eighth Grade* (New York: The Free Press, 1999).

12. Kindergarten readiness is of course a moving target, depending on changing expectations and standards as well as vast differences by topic, subject, and demographic group. A sophisticated Educational Testing Service study found that 65 percent of entering kindergartners in 1998 were able to recognize the letters of the alphabet while 93 percent could recognize numbers and shapes. But this ranged (for alphabet recognition) from 85 percent among tykes from the highest socioeconomic quintile to 39 percent among those in the lowest quintile. See Richard Coley, *An Uneven Start: Indicators of Inequality in School Readiness* (Princeton, N.J.: Educational Testing Service, 2002).

13. A vast amount of literature on this subject has been produced by many scholars, perhaps most famously Betty Hart and Todd Risley, whose 1995 book, *Meaningful Differences in the Everyday Experiences of Young American Children* (Baltimore: Paul H. Brookes Publishing, 1995), has had an enduring influence on our understanding of the knowledge with which kids do and don't enter school. For a concise version of their findings, see Hart and Risley, "The Early Catastrophe: The 30 Million Word Gap by Age 3," *American Educator*, Spring 2003, www.aft.org/pubs-reports/american_educator/spring2003/catastrophe.html.

14. G. Reid Lyon, "What Principals Need to Know About Reading," *Principal* 83, no. 2 (November-December 2003): 14-18. Lyon and others who make such estimates are, of course, referring to the total number of words the child will have heard, not the number of unique words. Thus a five-year-old may have heard "stop" or "love" a thousand times but "albatross" not even once.

15. As recounted in Clayton M. Christensen, Michael B. Horn, and Curtis W. Johnson, *Disrupting Class: How Disruptive Innovation Will Change the Way the World Learns* (New York: McGraw-Hill, 2008), pp. 149-53. Other credible analysts are far less gloomy about what can be accomplished, even with disadvantaged children, after they enter kindergarten or first grade—provided that schools do right by them. Reid

Lyon, for example, says that "The majority of children who enter kindergarten and first grade at risk for reading failure can learn to read at average or above-average levels—but only if they are identified early and provided with systematic, explicit, and intensive instruction in phonemic awareness, phonics, reading fluency, vocabulary, and reading comprehension strategies." See Lyon, "What Principals Need to Know About Reading."

16. Richard Barth, e-mail message to author, April 10, 2008.

17. E.D. Hirsch Jr., "Equity Effects of Very Early Schooling in France," Core Knowledge, http://coreknowledge.org/CK/Preschool/frenchequity.htm. For another view of the subject, see Bonnie R. Hurless, "Early Childhood Education in France: A Personal Perspective," National Association for the Education of Young Children, http://journal.naeyc.org/btj/200409/hurless.asp. Note that nursery schooling in France is government provided and operated and, though not compulsory, is universally available to all three- and four-year-olds, nearly all of whom take part in it; recently, some two-year-olds have also been enrolled. The research is not as clear cut as I, an English-only reader, would like. But it suggests higher achievement, as well as less likelihood of having to repeat a grade by grade five, for disadvantaged youngsters who start early.

18. E.D. Hirsch Jr., testimony before the Subcommittee on Children and Families of the Senate Committee on Labor, and the Subcommittee on Early Childhood, Youth, and Families of the House Committee on Education and the Workforce (joint hearing), 105th Cong., 2d sess., March 28, 1998, http://coreknowledge. org/CK/about/articles/headStartTestimony.htm.

19. See (among many possibilities) www.parentsasteachers.org; www.hippyusa. org; www.ed.gov/programs/evenstartformula/gtepevenstartformula.pdf; www.universal preschool.com,www.kidsparkz.com/index.html;www.ed.gov/parents/earlychild/ready/ edpicks.jhtml?src=ln; www2.scholastic.com/browse/schoolandlearning.jsp; and www. savvysource.com/educational_toys. Unfortunately, while parents have a huge impact on the educational readiness of their children, the effect of most parent-based intervention programs is modest. An Abt Associates evaluation of the federal Even Start program, for example, found no lasting educational result for children whose families participated in it. See Robert St. Pierre et al., *National Evaluation of the Even Start Family Literacy Plan* (Cambridge, Mass.: Abt Associates, 1995), www.abtassociates.com/reports/evenstart. pdf.

20. Joseph Epstein, "The Kindergarchy," *The Weekly Standard*, June 9, 2008, pp. 21-27.

21. This can be a mixed benefit. Jay Belsky, Robert Pianta, and other analysts, primarily working with data from the long-running NIH-sponsored "Study of Early Child Care and Youth Development," have found some evidence that extensive exposure

to center-based (rather than home-based) child-care during the early years is associated with more aggressive and acting-out behavior when youngsters reach school. See https://secc.rti.org/home.cfm.

22. My granddaughter, now five years old, has for several years been attending an upscale New York "preschool" of the traditional sort that seems to do a fine job of cognitive development but that, depending on the kids' ages, operates only three to five hours a day—and offers no after-school care. Hence parents must make a complete set of additional arrangements to pick their kids up at noon or 2 p.m. and look after them until Mom and Dad get home from work. It's a major hassle—and expensive, too.

23. Another NCES report yields slightly different numbers for four-year-olds in 2005-6: 20 percent with "no regular non parental arrangement"; 57.5 percent in "center-based" programs, of which about one-fifth were in Head Start; and 20.7 percent looked after in "home-based" arrangements with relatives or non-relatives. (An additional 1.9 percent were cared for under "multiple arrangements.") See U.S. Department of Education, National Center for Education Statistics, "Participation in Education," http://nces.ed.gov/programs/coe/2008/section1/table.asp?tableID=857.

24. Iheoma U. Iruka and Priscilla R. Carver, *Initial Results from the 2005 NHES Early Childhood Program Participation Survey*, U.S. Department of Education, NCES 2006-075 (Washington, D.C.: National Center for Education Statistics, 2006), p. 59, table 14.

25. Douglas J. Besharov and Douglas M. Call, "The New Kindergarten: The Case for Universal Pre-Kindergarten Isn't as Strong as It Seems," *Wilson Quarterly*, Autumn 2008, pp. 30-31.

26. NHES data indicate that 27 percent of three-through-five-year-olds have "no weekly nonparental care arrangement." Iruka and Carver, *Initial Results*, p. 7, table 1.

27. Indiana's Family and Social Service Administration explains that "CCDF direct service dollars are to provide financial assistance to eligible TANF and low income families in need of child care. Parents can choose from available licensed or legally license-exempt child care. Types of care might include: center-based care, school-age care, in-home care, relative care, and sectarian child care. All child care providers must meet applicable state and local requirements including CCDF Provider Eligibility Standards." (TANF refers to the federal Temporary Assistance to Needy Families program that replaced AFDC in the aftermath of the 1996 welfare reform.) See Indiana Family and Social Service Administration, Division of Family Resources, *CCDF Voucher Program Policy and Procedures Manual* (revised

September 29, 2008), p. 3, www.in.gov/fssa/files/CCDFPolicyProcedureManual v10-07__rev_9-29-08_.pdf.

28. Douglas J. Besharov, Caeli A. Higney, and Justus A. Myers, *Federal and State Child Care and Early Education Expenditures, 1997-2005: Child Care Spending Falls as Pre-K Spending Rises* (Washington, D.C.: Welfare Reform Academy, 2007), p. 4, table 1. The category labeled "state-funded pre-K" is, of course, the sum of a number of separate state programs.

29. National Institute for Early Education Research, *The State of Preschool 2007: State Preschool Yearbook* (New Brunswick, N.J.: Rutgers University, 2007), p. 10.

30. These include both "nursery school" and "kindergarten," the definitions of which are, frankly, a bit hazy.

31. The profound effect that James S. Coleman's monumental 1966 study, *On Equality of Educational Opportunity*, has had on American primary-secondary education over the past four decades is sketched in my book, *Troublemaker: A Personal History of School Reform Since Sputnik* (Princeton, N.J.: Princeton University Press, 2008), pp. 18-19, 46-47, 101-102 and 200-201. See also Debra Viadero, "Race Report's Influence Felt 40 Years Later," *Education Week*, June 21, 2006, http://www.edweek.org/ew/articles/2006/06/21/41coleman.h25.html.

32. For example, see David Blau and Janet Currie, "Preschool, Day Care, and After-School Care: Who's Minding the Kids?" in Eric Hanushek and Finis Welch, eds., *Handbook of the Economics of Education*, Handbooks in Economics, no. 26 (Amsterdam: North-Holland Press, 2006), 2: 1183-184.

33. Albert Shanker Institute, *Preschool Curriculum: What's in It for Children and Teachers* (Washington, D.C.: Albert Shanker Institute, 2009), p. 2.

34. Jean I. Layzer and Barbara D. Goodson, "The 'Quality' of Early Care and Education Settings," *Evaluation Review* 30 (October 2006): 570.

35. See, for example, Diane M. Early et al., "Teachers' Education, Classroom Quality, and Young Children's Academic Skills: Results from Seven Studies of Preschool Programs," *Child Development* 78 (March-April 2007): 558-80.

36. Deborah L. Cohen, "Goals Panel Adopts Plan to Develop Early-Childhood Assessment System," *Education Week*, April 8, 1992, www.edweek.org/ew/articles/1992/04/08/29goals.h11.html

37. Martha Zaslow et al., "Child Outcome Measures in the Study of Child Care Quality," *Evaluation Review* 30 (October 2006): 592, table 3.

38. Blau and Currie, "Preschool, Day Care, and After-School Care," pp. 1183-184.

39. A good description of Pianta's classroom-level observation system, the criteria it uses, and much of what's been learned by deploying it, can be found at www.classobservation.com/what/index.php.

40. Robert C. Pianta, "Preschool is School, Sometimes," *Education Next* 7 (Winter 2007), www.hoover.org/publications/ednext/4612287.html.

41. Blau and Currie, "Preschool, Day Care, and After-School Care," p. 1195.

42. Andrew J. Mashburn et al., "Measures of Classroom Quality in Prekindergarten and Children's Development of Academic, Language, and Social Skills," *Child Development* 79 (May-June 2008): 732-49.

43. Linda Jacobson, "Teacher-Pupil Link Crucial to Pre-K Success, Study Says," *Education Week*, May 28, 2008, p. 9, www.edweek.org/ew/articles/2008/05/21/38early.h27.html?qs=Linda+Jacobson.

44. E.D. Hirsch Jr., *The Schools We Need and Why We Don't Have Them* (New York: Doubleday, 1996), p. 79. Hirsch cites as examples of "expert attacks" on structured early learning two books by David Elkind, *The Hurried Child: Growing Up Too Fast Too Soon* (Cambridge, Mass.: Perseus Publishing, 2001); and *Miseducation: Preschoolers at Risk* (New York: Alfred A. Knopf, 1987).

45. Iruka and Carver, *Initial Results*, p. 63, table 15.

46. See *Troublemaker*, chaps. 23-24.

47. Bruce Fuller, *Standardized Childhood: The Political and Cultural Struggle over Early Education* (Stanford: Stanford University Press, 2007), pp. 208-9. How to interpret "effect sizes" like these is a constant conundrum. By one reasonable interpretation, raising student achievement by a quarter of a standard deviation equates roughly to a half year more of school in the early grades.

48. Figlio and Roth, "The Behavioral Consequences of Pre-Kindergarten," p. 29.

49. Jill S. Cannon, Alison Jacknowitz, and Gary Painter, "Is Full Better than Half? Examining the Longitudinal Effects of Full-Day Kindergarten Attendance" (working paper, RAND Labor and Population series, 2005), http://rand.org/pubs/working_papers/2005/RAND_WR266-1.pdf.

50. Fuller, *Standardized Childhood*, p. 284.

51. Ibid., p. 225.

52. Douglas J. Besharov, "Preschool Puzzle," *Education Next* 8 (Fall 2008), www.hoover.org/publications/ednext/27149734.html.

53. Fuller, *Standardized Childhood*, p. 193.

54. Douglas J. Besharov et al., "Summaries of Twenty-Four Early Childhood Evaluations" (unpublished manuscript, July, 2008), p. 4.

55. Michael L. Anderson, "Multiple Inference and Gender Differences in the Effects of Early Intervention: A Reevaluation of the Abecedarian, Perry Preschool, and Early Training Projects," *Journal of the American Statistical Association* 103 (December

1, 2008): 1481-495, http://129.3.20.41/eps/hew/papers/0509/0509008.pdf.

56. Searching for long-term effects of Head Start, Eliana Garces, Duncan Thomas and Janet Currie found that the program's effects were more likely to fade among African American youngsters than among white Head Start graduates and speculated that the cause is "that African American children who attended Head Start go on to attend schools of lower quality than other African American children." Garces, Thomas, and Currie, "Longer Term Effects of Head Start," *American Economic Review* 92 (September 2002): 999-1012.

57. One might think this problem would gradually disappear as pre-K participation becomes more universal. But until and unless it becomes *compulsory*, that isn't likely to happen. Experience so far indicates that 50-70 percent of four-year-olds are apt to take part in a state-financed "universal" program.

58. After extensive observation of elementary school classrooms, Robert Pianta and his research team concluded that, even for middle-class youngsters, teaching was "geared toward performance of basic reading and math skills, not problem-solving or reasoning skills or other content areas....[S]tudents most in need of high-quality instruction are unlikely to experience it consistently." Pianta et al., "Opportunities to Learn in America's Elementary Classrooms," *Science*, March 30, 2007, p. 1796.

59. The June 2008 draft can be viewed at www.fldoe.org/earlylearning/pdf/2008EdustandFinJune.pdf.

60. VPK arithmetic assessments are also being developed—in number sense and geometry—for statewide use in the 2010-11 school year.

61. Florida Department of Education, 2008 Voluntary Prekindergarten Education Standards, www.fldoe.org/earlylearning/pdf/vpkedstandard.pdf.

62. Early Learning Success Initiative, "Building a Strong Foundation for Florida's Children: Early Success in Reading and Math" (presentation at Florida State Board of Education meeting, April 15, 2008), www.fldoe.org/board/meetings/2008_04_15/Early%20Learning%20Success.pdf.

63. At present, these are a subset of the Early Childhood Observation System and the Letter Naming Fluency and Initial Sound Fluency measures from the Dynamic Indicators of Basic Early Literacy Skills (DIBELS). The Florida Center for Reading Research is developing new teacher-administered reading assessments, intended to replace DIBELS by 2009-10. Also under development are new VPK assessments of alphabetic knowledge, phonological awareness, and vocabulary that are to be aligned with the new kindergarten assessments and ready for use by 2010-11.

64. Florida Legislature, Office of Program Policy Analysis and Government Accountability, Report no. 08-23 (Tallahassee, Fla., April 2008), www.oppaga.state.fl.us/reports/pdf/0823rpt.pdf.

65. See https://vpk.fldoe.org/Default.aspx.

66. Kirp, *The Sandbox Investment*, pp. 192-94.

67. David McKay Wilson, "When Worlds Collide: Universal PreK Brings New Challenges for Public Elementary Schools," *Harvard Education Letter*, November-December 2008, p. 2.

68. Lyndon B. Johnson, "Letter to the President of the Senate and to the Speaker of the House on Stepping Up the War on Poverty," February 17, 1965, www.presidency.ucsb.edu/ws/index.php?pid=27432. The background and launch of Head Start are well covered in Maris A. Vinovskis, *The Birth of Head Start: Preschool Education Policies in the Kennedy and Johnson Administrations* (Chicago: University of Chicago Press, 2005).

69. Lyndon B. Johnson, "Remarks on Head Start," May 18, 1965, www.presidency.ucsb.edu/ws/index.php?pid=26973&st=Johnson&st1=.

70. Ironically, advocates' efforts to deny that Head Start is an education program may have masked such evidence as there is—modest, to be sure, but not nil—that the program has some lasting positive effects in the education sphere, such as an increased likelihood, at least for white youngsters, of completing high school and going on to college. See Garces, Thomas, and Currie, "Longer Term Effects of Head Start."

71. Hirsch, *The Schools We Need*, pp. 45-46.

72. Edward Zigler and Susan Muenchow, *Head Start: The Inside Story of America's Most Successful Educational Experiment* (New York: Basic Books, 1993), p. 83.

73. A number of other programs that might reasonably be categorized as "education" – such as Indian Education, the school lunch program, and the Defense Department's schools for military dependents – also didn't make it into the new department. I recount this tale in chapter 7 of *Troublemaker*.

74. Edward Zigler, "The Wrong Read on Head Start," *New York Times*, December 23, 2000.

75. U.S. Department of Health and Human Services, Administration for Children and Families, *Head Start Impact Study: First Year Findings* (Washington, D.C., 2005).

76. Results were, as Douglas Besharov and Caeli Higney acknowledge, a bit better for three-year-olds. See *Giving Head Start a Fresh Start* (Washington, D.C.: Welfare Reform Academy, 2007), p. 3.

77. Muddying this picture, NIEER is in this case not simply counting explicit state-level outlays for programs labeled pre-K or preschool but estimating total

public funding from all sources—including local and federal as well as multi-state programs—expended on behalf of pre-K programs operating under state auspices.

78. Bruce Fuller reports that the true cost of the Abecedarian Project, expressed in 2000 dollars, was $34,476 per child. Fuller, *Standardized Childhood*, p. 195.

79. Henry M. Levin and Heather L. Schwartz, "What is the Cost of a Preschool Program?" (paper presented at the American Education Finance Association annual conference, Baltimore, March 23, 2007).

80. Adding very young children would actually boost the cost quite a lot more because state regulations always stipulate significantly richer staff-to-children ratios for babies and toddlers.

81. Kirp, *The Sandbox Investment*, p. 87.

82. Fuller, *Standardized Childhood*, p. 195.

83. John F. Witte, "A Proposal for State, Income-Targeted Preschool Vouchers," *Peabody Journal of Education* 82, no. 4 (October 2007): 22. The University of Virginia's Robert Pianta also favors targeting pre-K programs at 150 to 200% of the federal poverty line; he cites evidence that such youngsters often fare poorly in school and that well-crafted pre-K programs show promising results with them.

84. Clive R. Belfield, "Early Childhood Education: How Important Are the Cost-Savings to the School System?" (report prepared for the Center for Early Care and Education, 2004).

85. Analyses such as Belfield's and Heckman's are thoughtfully debunked—in the California context— in Chris Cardiff and Edward Stringham, *Is Universal Preschool Beneficial?: An Analysis of RAND Corporation's Analysis and Proposals for California* (Los Angeles: Reason Foundation, 2006), www.reason.org/ps345_universal preschool.pdf.

86. Fuller, *Standardized Childhood*, p. 60.

87. National Education Association, *NEA on Prekindergarten and Kindergarten* (Washington, D.C.: National Education Association, 2004), p. 6, www.nea.org/assets/docs/mf_prekkinder.pdf.

88. See Council of Chief State School Officers, Early Childhood and Family Education (Washington, D.C.: Council of Chief State School Officers, 1999), p.5, www.ccsso.org/content/pdfs/Early_Childhood_Policy_99.pdf.

89. There is a wide range, however – from 14 percent in Michigan to 93 percent in the District of Columbia (2005). See p. 9, table II.2 in Gretchen Kirby and Andrew Burwick, *Using Vouchers to Deliver Social Services: Considerations Based on the Child Care and Development Fund (CCDF) and Temporary Assistance for Needy Families (TANF) Program Experiences* (Washington, D.C.: Mathematica Policy Research, 2007).

90. In 2005, California, for example, estimated its waiting list at 280,000 children. For a relatively lucid explanation of how this complex program works, Indiana's Children's Bureau has helpful information on its website. See www.childrensbureau. org/html/ccdf.cfm.

91. Kirby and Burwick, *Using Vouchers to Deliver Social Services*, pp. 41-43.

92. Witte, "A Proposal," pp. 22-25. For Witte's appraisal of K–12 vouchers in Milwaukee, see his *The Market Approach to Education: An Analysis of America's First Voucher Program* (Princeton, N.J.: Princeton University Press, 2001).

93. Fuller, *Standardized Childhood*, p. 285.

94. A perennial topic in all discussions of vouchers is whether users should be able to supplement them with their own money. That may not be feasible for low income participants, but it is for those with more money—and of course the latter could squeeze the former out of "slots" in the most attractive programs, which might charge as much as the market will bear.

95. Pre-K Now, "Community-Based Pre-K Providers," www.preknow.org/ educators/providers.cfm.

96. Fuller, *Standardized Childhood*, pp. xv-xix.

97. Incorporating pre-K programs into school system operations turns out to entail wrenching changes that not all of them can successfully make. See David McKay Wilson, "When Worlds Collide."

98. Fuller, *Standardized Childhood*, p. 223.

99. Florida's public-school systems are required to offer summer VPK programs but not the school-year version. Overall, school systems comprise less then 20 percent of all VPK providers in the state. But the Miami-Dade system, which has heartily embraced this approach, is by far the largest VPK provider in Florida.

100. Tim Craig, "Kaine Trims Pre-K Proposal," *Washington Post*, August 17, 2007, p. B01, www.washingtonpost.com/wp-dyn/content/article/2007/08/16/AR20070 81602518.html.

101. See, for example, the website of Preschool California at www.preschool california.org/about-us/mission-and-work.html.

102. Sara Mead, "Obama's $10 Billion Early Childhood Education Pledge," *Washington Times*, December 28, 2008.

103. Although it's next to impossible to gauge the size of such a "windfall," RAND analysts estimated that, in California, at least half of the measure's $2.4 billion annual cost "would go to families who already could afford to pay for preschool." The *Los Angeles Times* editorialized that "in order to pay for 25,000 to 50,000 additional children in preschool, taxpayers would foot the bill for the 325,000 other four-year-olds already in preschool." Fuller, *Standardized Childhood*, pp. 175-76.

104. More precisely, one can draw reasonably clear and definitive conclusions from various studies that differ dramatically from one another. See, for example, Linda Jacobson, "New Analysis Bolsters Child Care, Behavior Link," *Education Week*, April 4, 2007, www.edweek.org/ew/articles/2007/04/04/31nichd_side.h26. html?qs=child+care; and Linda Jacobson, "Studies Find Payoffs, Drawbacks Persist for Pupils in Preschool and Child Care," *Education Week*, November 2, 2005, www. edweek.org/ew/articles/2005/11/02/10care.h25.html.

105. Cardiff and Stringham, *Is Universal Preschool Beneficial?*

106. As Fuller, Besharov and others have noted, some countries have fruitfully focused their early-childhood assistance efforts as much on maternity/paternity leave for new parents, part-time work and job-sharing options, and home-support programs of various kinds as on center-based and school-based programs.

107. "Targeting" doesn't necessarily have to be income-based. Besharov suggests using various indicators of "risk" to the child, such as having a young single mother.

108. That history is recounted in various places including Eric Haney, *The Follow Through Planned Variation Experiment*, vol. 5, *A Technical History of the National Follow Through Evaluation* (Cambridge, Mass.: Huron Institute, 1977); Cathy L. Watkins, "Follow Through: Why Didn't We?" *Effective School Practices* 15 (Winter 1995-96), www.uoregon.edu/~adiep/ft/watkins.htm; and Maris A. Vinovskis, *History and Educational Policymaking* (New Haven, Conn.: Yale University Press, 1999), esp. chap. 4.

109. See Minnesota Early Learning Foundation, *Annual Report* (St. Paul, Minn.: Minnesota Early Learning Foundation, 2008), www.melf.us/vertical/Sites/ %7B3D4B6DDA-94F7-44A4-899D-3267CBEB798B%7D/uploads/ %7B3376243D-DAF1-48F2-8D1E-11D4BCBD010E%7D.PDF. The foundation is interesting in part because it's one of many results of the efforts made by Art Rolnick, an analyst at the Minneapolis Federal Reserve Bank, to call attention to early-childhood education as a smart societal investment. But rather than simply embracing a "universal pre-K" model, the Minnesota business leaders and others who responded opted to undertake a series of careful studies, pilot programs, rival models and careful evaluations in this area, including programs that help needy parents become more effective in their own homes and more sophisticated and informed consumers of center-based offerings.

110. I find considerable merit in Besharov's proposal to intensify Head Start's cognitive focus and target the program more precisely on the most acutely disadvantaged young children, as well as to provide additional services and interventions for parents, even beginning during pregnancy. See Besharov and Higney, *Giving Head Start a Fresh Start*, esp. pp. 13-15.

111. States might opt to develop a two-tier licensure system, one intended for pure "day care" programs, with operators and programs so labeled, the other for "preschool" programs. Perhaps operators would have to satisfy the latter criteria—and take part in a related results-based accountability system, with transparent public reporting—in order to use the word "school" or "preschool" in their names and marketing materials.

112. See, for example, my book, *Troublemaker*; Terry M. Moe, *A Primer on America's Schools* (Stanford: Hoover Institution Press, 2001); Paul E. Peterson, *Our Schools and Our Future...Are We Still at Risk?* (Stanford: Hoover Institution Press, 2003); and John E. Chubb, *Within Our Reach: How America Can Educate Every Child* (Lanham, Md.: Rowman & Littlefield, 2005).

113. James J. Heckman, "Beyond Pre-K: Rethinking Conventional Wisdom on Eduational Intervention," Erie Neighborhood House, March 19, 2007, http://eriehouse.org/article.asp?objectTypeID=11&objectID=1143.

# About the Author

**Chester E. Finn, Jr.** is president of the Thomas B. Fordham Institute, senior editor of *Education Next*, senior fellow at Stanford's Hoover Institution and chairman of Hoover's Task Force on K–12 Education. For 40 years, he has been in the forefront of the national debate about school reform

Finn previously served as founding partner of the Edison Project, Professor of Education and Public Policy at Vanderbilt University, Assistant Secretary for Research and Improvement at the U.S. Department of Education, Staff Assistant to the President of the United States, Special Assistant to the Governor of Massachusetts, Counsel to the U.S. Ambassador to India, Research Associate at the Brookings Institution and Legislative Director for Senator Daniel Patrick Moynihan.

Previous books include *Troublemaker: A Personal History of School Reform Since Sputnik; No Remedy Left Behind*, co-edited with Frederick M. Hess; *Leaving No Child Behind: Options for Kids in Failing Schools*, also co-edited with Hess; *Charter Schools in Action: Renewing Public Education*, co-authored with Bruno V. Manno and Gregg Vanourek; and *The Educated Child: A Parent's Guide from Pre-School Through Eighth Grade*, co-authored with William J. Bennett and John Cribb. He has also authored more than 400 articles in leading journals and newspapers.

A native of Ohio, he holds an undergraduate degree in U.S. history, a master's degree in social studies teaching, and a doctorate in education policy, all from Harvard University. He and his wife, Renu Virmani, a physician, have two grown children and two adorable pre-school granddaughters. They live in Chevy Chase, Maryland.

# Index

Abecedarian Project, 86; as boutique or hothouse program, 47, 75; cost per participant in, 49, 109n78; long-term effects of, 48, 49

academic achievement: closing gaps in, 3, 4, 7, 12, 15–16; fade out in gains from early education programs, 45–51; in Head Start, 67, 69; initial impact of pre-K education on, 44; kindergarten programs affecting, 45–46; precursor skills required for, 9–10; in public schools, 82–83; in targeted intensive programs, 7

administration of pre-K programs, as factor in quality assessment, 34

African-American children: in Abecedarian Project, 48; assessment of educational progress, 82; in Head Start, 107n56; in Oklahoma preschool programs, 63; population of, 87; targeted programs for, 86

Albert Shanker Institute, 31

alphabet recognition: in Head Start, 69; in kindergarten readiness, 102n12

Anderson, Michael, 48

Arizona, state pre-K spending per child in, 72

Barnett, Steve, 76

Barth, Richard, 17

behavior: of disadvantaged low-income children, 10–11, 44; in Head Start, 68; participation in pre-K programs affecting, 10–11, 44, 46, 103–104n21

Belfield, Clive, 76

Bennett, William J., 13–14, 82

Besharov, Douglas, 69, 83, 91; on Abecedarian Project, 47, 48; on cognitive gains in Head Start, 69; on demand for universal pre-K programs, 26–27; on funding of pre-K programs, 28, 101n4; on Perry Preschool, 47; on public school pre-K programs, 6

black children. See African-American children

Blaine amendments, 80

Blau, David, 36, 37–38

"broader, bolder" approach to education, 3, 101n5

Building Blocks (Maeroff), 5

Burwick, Andrew, 80

Bush, George W., 68

Bush, Jeb, 53

California, 109n85, 110n90; kindergarten content standards in, 102n10; pre-K advocacy movement in, 88; Rob Reiner initiative in, 5, 88, 91; windfall effect of proposed universal pre-K program in, 91, 102n103

Call, Douglas, 6, 26

CCDF. See Child Care and Development Fund

center-based programs: behavioral effects of, 44; population of children in, 24, 25, 25f, 104n23

Chicago: Child-Parent Center in, 48–49, 75; preschool population in, 1–2

child care. See day care

# EDUCATION
## next
### B O O K S

EDUCATION NEXT BOOKS address major subjects related to efforts to reform American public education. This imprint features assessments and monographs by Hoover Institution fellows (including members of the Hoover Institution's Task Force on K–12 Education), as well as those of outside experts.

*Advancing Student Achievement*
Herbert J. Walberg
*(published by Education Next Books, 2009)*

*Learning from No Child Left Behind:
How and Why the Nation's Most
Important but Controversial Education
Law Should Be Renewed*
John E. Chubb
*(published by Education Next Books, 2009)*

*Reroute the Preschool Juggernaut*
Chester E. Finn, Jr.
*(published by Education Next Books, 2009)*

*Courting Failure:
How School Finance Lawsuits Exploit
Judges' Good Intentions and Harm Our
Children*
Edited by Eric A. Hanushek
*(published by Education Next Books, 2006)*

*Charter Schools against the Odds*
Edited by Paul T. Hill
*(published by Education Next Books, 2006)*

*Within Our Reach:
How America Can Educate Every Child*
Edited by John E. Chubb
*(published by Rowman & Littlefield, 2005)*

*Our Schools and Our Future
...Are We Still at Risk?*
Edited by Paul E. Peterson
*(published by Hoover Institution Press, 2003)*

*Choice with Equity*
Edited by Paul T. Hill
*(published by Hoover Institution Press, 2002)*

*School Accountability*
Edited by Williamson M. Evers and
Herbert J. Walberg
*(published by Hoover Institution Press, 2002)*

*A Primer on America's Schools*
Edited by Terry M. Moe
*(published by Hoover Institution Press, 2001)*

OF RELATED INTEREST:
*Education and Capitalism:
How Overcoming Our Fear of
Markets and Economics Can Improve
America's Schools*
Edited by Herbert J. Walberg and
Joseph L. Bast
*(published by Hoover Institution Press, 2003)*